The Passion of Jesus
in the
Gospel of Mark

The Passion Series

Volume 2

The Passion of Jesus in the Gospel of Mark

by

Donald Senior, C.P.

Michael Glazier, Inc.

Wilmington, Delaware

About the Author:
Donald Senior, C.P., is Professor of New Testament at
Catholic Theological Union in Chicago. He has written
extensively on biblical subjects. Among his publications are
*The Passion Narrative According to Matthew; Jesus: A
Gospel Portrait* and *1 & 2 Peter*, volume 20 of the New
Testament Message series, of which he is co-editor. He is
also a book review editor for *The Catholic Biblical
Quarterly.*

First published in 1984 by Michael Glazier, Inc., 1723 Delaware Avenue,
Wilmington, Delaware, 19806.

Library of Congress Cataloging in Publication Data

Senior, Donald.
    The Passion of Jesus in the Gospel of Mark.

    Includes index.
    1. Jesus Christ — Passion. 2. Bible. N.T. Mark—
Criticism, interpretation, etc. I. Title.
BT431.S46 1984   226'.306   84-81248
ISBN 0-89453-436-X

Cover design by Lillian Brulc. The crucifix used on pages 2, 4 and
cover IV by Eric Gill©.

Printed in the United States of America

CONTENTS

5

PREFACE

No one is a stranger to suffering. Pain touches every human being, regardless of nationality, social standing, ideology, or personal integrity. Suffering is both individual and communal. Sickness can drain a single body just as fear, violence or poverty can waste a nation. Death comes as the ultimate suffering, bringing termination to even the most tranquil of human lives.

The struggle to understand the origin and meaning of suffering is as long as human history. It is not surprising, therefore, that the suffering and death of Jesus should have such a prominent place in the Gospels. Each of the Gospels revolves around the crucifixion of Jesus. This interest, as we shall discuss at length in the chapters that follow, was not simply in the dramatic historical fact that Jesus of Nazareth was publicly executed by crucifixion. Rather, the evangelists sought the meaning of all this, not only for Jesus' life but for all human life. How could this happen? And what purpose might it have? These were the questions that drew Christians to Jesus' death. Discovering coherence in the sufferings of Jesus might yield the meaning of suffering in their own lives.

Christians speak of the "passion" of Jesus. The subtle layers of meaning in the word help illustrate something else that is at stake here. "Passion" derives from the Latin word *patior* and it means to "suffer," "endure," "bear." When we speak of Christ's "passion," we refer, of course, to the suffering and death that he endured. But "passion" has other connotations in English. It can mean intense emotion, feeling, even commitment. People can do things "with a passion." Both sides of the term "passion" come into play in the Gospels. Jesus of Nazareth was condemned to die; the cross was imposed on him. He was in this sense a victim of suffering and death, just as every human being is. But the other side of "passion" is present too. The crucifixion was no surprise, falling on Jesus like a tile off a roof. The Gospels make it clear that the hostility against Jesus was a result of Jesus' own mission. Because of his unyielding commitment, his "passion," Jesus put himself on a collision course with certain powerful forces in society. From this perspective Jesus' death was the outcome of his life; he "chose" death. In the language of the gospel, he "took up the cross."

Recent Christian experience (and recent theology in its wake) has grasped in a new way these two dimensions of the cross. The cross is both what we have to endure and what we actively and deliberately take up. In the martyr churches of Latin America or China or Eastern Europe there are many Christians who continue to bear suffering — the sick, the elderly, the dying. But there are many others who take up the cross by risking suffering and violent death in the pursuit of justice.

The "Passion of Jesus" referred to in this book implies both the passive and active dimensions of human suffering.

It would be arrogant folly to suggest that what follows will "solve" the riddle of suffering. The passion narratives do not offer packaged answers to the questions created by human agony. But they do offer perspective and meaning. They show Jesus, Son of God and child of the universe, walking the same path of pain and death, yet not broken by it. They portray this representative human, this "new Adam," displaying the many moods of the Christian before death: anguish, lament, peaceful acceptance, stunned silence. They invite the reader to locate his or her place in the cast of characters who swirl through the drama — the hostile opponents, the betrayer, the terrorized disciples, a leader who denies, the vacillating crowd, the women who stand boldly present at the cross. The narratives place all of this drama on the stage of biblical history. The voices of the prophets, the anguished prayers of the psalmist and many other texts of the Hebrew Bible were drawn into the passion story to help the early church detect the pattern of God's presence, even here in what seemed the darkest moment of human history. By retelling the passion story and placing themselves in it, the early Christians found new coherence in their own passion. Through liturgy, drama, and personal reflection generation after generation of believers have done the same.

Contemporary biblical scholarship is divided over exactly how the passion story developed.[1] In earlier decades, scholars were confident that the passion story had enjoyed independent existence prior to the writing of the Gospels. They observed that the passion, especially from the arrest of Jesus on, was the only place in the Gospels where all four evangelists are in significant harmony. And the passion is an extended, coherent narrative, unlike the more staccato structure of the rest of the gospel materials. The passion therefore would have been the earliest part of the gospel tradition to take shape. Some suggested this was prompted by the need to explain how Jesus had died and how this was in conformity with God's will and with the Hebrew Scriptures. The paradox of proclaiming as God's Son one who had been rejected by his own people and publicly executed by the Roman State (and by a means of execution usually reserved for sedition) would surely call for explanation to Jew and Gentile alike.[2]

---

[1] Cf. the discussion in J. Donahue, "From Passion Traditions to Passion Narrative," in W. Kelber (ed.), *The Passion in Mark* (Philadelphia: Fortress, 1976), 1-20; also F. Matera, *The Kingship of Jesus: Composition and Theology in Mark 15* (SBL Dissertation Series 66; Chico, CA: Scholars Press, 1982), 1-5.

[2] A representative of this position would be Martin Dibelius in his groundbreaking work, *From Tradition to Gospel* (New York: Scribners, N.D.), 178-217. This is an English translation of a study that originally appeared in 1919.

Others suggest that the liturgy would have been the likely setting for the origin of the earliest passion narrative.[3] In a context of communal worship, perhaps even a vigil service commemorating the Lord's death, the story would have been retold and blended with prayer and reflection upon the Hebrew Scriptures. This might explain the strong influence of the psalms and other biblical texts on the language of the passion story.

However, more recent scholarship has questioned the existence of any coherent passion narrative prior to Mark's Gospel. If, as most scholars suppose, Mark was the first Gospel to be written, it is not surprising that the question of a pre-existing passion story is most critical in discussions of this Gospel.

Some recent interpreters of Mark continue to maintain that part or most of the passion account was formed prior to Mark. In a massive commentary on the Gospel, Rudolph Pesch asserts that the evangelist had access to a complete passion story that would have begun with Jesus' journey to Jerusalem (in Mark's Gospel, the scene at Caesarea Philippi, 8:27) and extended through the entire story of Jesus' confrontation with his opponents in Jerusalem and the passion account itself.[4] According to Pesch, this passion narrative developed very early in the Jerusalem Christian community and had a strong degree of historical reliability. Mark incorporated the account into his Gospel with only minimal changes.

Other scholars would be less bold than Pesch, but would suggest that substantial elements of the passion story were already in place prior to Mark and were re-worked by Mark the evangelist as he incorporated them into his Gospel.[5]

---

[3] This was proposed by G. Bertram, *Die Leidensgeschichte und der Christuskult* (FRLANT 22: Göttingen: Vandenhoeck & Ruprecht, 1922).

[4] R. Pesch, *Das Markusevangelium* (Herders Theologischer Kommentar zum Neuen Testament; Freiburg/Basel/Wien: Herder, 3rd revised ed., 1980; 2 vols.). A detailed exposition of Pesch's views on the pre-Markan passion story can be found in volume 2, 1-27.

[5] One of the most ambitious attempts to reconstruct the tradition prior to Mark is that of Detlev Dormeyer who detects at least two stages of the Passion tradition previous to Mark's version; cf. *Die Passion Jesu als Verhaltensmodell* (NTAbh NF 11; Münster: Aschendorff, 1974).

On the other side of the spectrum are those who believe that little, if any, of the passion story was formed prior to Mark. Most of the authors in the collection, *The Passion in Mark*, for example, attribute full creativity to the evangelist.[6] He and he alone is responsible for the story of Jesus' death, a story that harmonizes with the style and theology of Mark throughout his Gospel.

Clearly some mediating position should be sought between these two radically different perspectives. Given the importance of Jesus' death in early Christian preaching, it is likely that the basic story would have taken shape prior to Mark and would have been known to him as it was to every Christian. However, Mark seems to have boldly retold the story in his own way. As the study that follows will illustrate, the language, tone and message of Mark's passion narrative blends with his entire portrayal of Jesus. The passion does not appear to be grafted on the Gospel but is the integral climax of all that has preceded.

The interest of this book is not to resolve this exegetical debate. But these discussions do offer us some important insights. The passion story was never a police blotter report on the final hours of Jesus' death. Instead, it was kneaded together in the faith life of the early church. Whatever the shape of the story prior to Mark (and there may have been several versions), it must have been imprinted with Christian experience as well as historical memory. Mark, in turn, felt free to retell and reinterpret that story for his own time and place. The passion of Jesus was not only a story from the past but, in the sufferings and hopes of the Christians, was a living reality of the present.

The purpose of this detailed examination of the Passion of Jesus in Mark is to invite the reader to experience in a new way the power of this narrative. As such, it is written for all those who are interested in Scripture and willing to read it closely. Because the four passion narratives have a remarkable degree of similarity and yet each bears the evident trade-

6 W. Kelber (ed.), *The Passion in Mark*. This series of essays was contributed by a group of American scholars who were influenced by the late Norman Perrin of the University of Chicago. This "Chicago school" gave strong emphasis to the creativity of Mark.

marks of its author, they are an excellent place to demonstrate the techniques and value of critical biblical scholarship. I hope, too, that the theological reflection emanating from a close reading of the passion story will be of use to those involved in pastoral ministry.

I make no apologies for linking exegesis of the biblical text with pastoral issues. The Bible cannot stand on its own. The biblical Word must be understood in the light of the Word as it is lived in the church. There is a deep kinship between modern pastoral issues and the biblical text, even though they are separated by time and culture. The Bible itself is "pastoral," that is, shaped by and directed to the faith life of the communities of Israel and the early church. Purely technical questions about language, literary forms or historical context all have an integral part to play in responsible interpretation. But ultimately the most fruitful insights, even into the original meaning of a biblical text — come when the interpreter is willing to relate life issues to the Bible. This is certainly the case when the texts at issue are the passion narratives.

This study is also directed to my colleagues in the biblical guild. Even though for the sake of a wider audience I have tried to avoid technical jargon and have minimized footnotes, these studies are, I hope, not a simplified version of someone else's research. My debt to ongoing biblical scholarship is evident and acknowledged. But these narratives have been a special focus of my own research for the past decade so I have attempted to put forth my own reading of the text as well as to dialogue with the interpretation of others.

Each volume in this four volume series will follow a similar format. An opening section introduces the material and shows how the passion story is prepared for in the body of Mark's Gospel. The second and dominant section is a detailed analysis of the passion narrative itself. The concluding section synthesizes the motifs or characteristics of the passion story, relates them to the overall theology of Mark and suggests possible implications for contemporary experience.

This series has a long genealogy. My introduction to a critical study of the passion narratives began at the University of Louvain where I completed my doctoral work on the passion narrative of Matthew in 1972 under the direction of Prof. Frans Neirynck. For the past ten years that apprenticeship bore fruit in a course I have taught on the passion narratives at Catholic Theological Union in Chicago. It was through the participants in that course that I was able to see the close connection between the passion stories and contemporary issues of suffering. The immediate stimulus for putting pen to paper was the encouragement of Michael Glazier, whose friendship and professional collaboration has been a joy to me for the past few years. I am also grateful to Ann Maloney, O.P. who shepherded the manuscript through its several drafts, and to Kenneth O'Malley, C.P., Director of the Catholic Theological Union Library, who prepared the indexes with the assistance of Penny Gorbach, O.P. and Therese Sachnik, O.P.

No influence has been more decisive for this project than the spirit of the religious community with whom I have lived and been nourished for more than twenty years. To my brother Passionists I gratefully dedicate this work.

PART I

PREPARATION FOR THE PASSION

Introduction

Mark's passion narrative begins in chapter 14 of the Gospel, but long before that point in the story is reached the reader is prepared for Jesus' death. The cross is not a stunning surprise; its shadow falls across the entire span of Jesus' ministry. By weaving allusions to the passion into the body of his Gospel, Mark illustrates the inner connection between Jesus' ministry and his death on the cross.

That connection is a major interest of contemporary christology.[1] The cross is not an arbitrary final act in the Jesus drama. It takes on meaning from the commitment of Jesus' life and vision. Mark's Gospel demonstrates how the character of Jesus' ministry *provoked* the opposition and misunderstanding that built into a hostile death-dealing force. The Jesus of Mark's Gospel is no mere victim, passively accepting an unjust death. He "takes up the cross," not by morbidly choosing death, but by choosing a way of life that would ultimately clash with those who could not see Jesus' way as God's way.

[1] See, for example, E. Schillebeeckx, *Jesus: An Experiment in Christology* (New York: Seabury, 1979), 294-319; H. Küng, *On Being a Christian* (New York: Doubleday, 1976), 319-42; W. Kasper, *Jesus the Christ* (New York: Paulist, 1976), 113-23; J. Sobrino, *Christology at the Crossroads* (Maryknoll, NY: Orbis, 1978), 201-04.

In this chapter we will look at several ways Mark prepares the reader for the passion. Each motif uncovered will explode in the passion story itself.

I. The Passion of the Baptist

In all four Gospels the haunting figure of John the Baptist serves as preparation for the mission of Jesus. He is the last of the prophets standing on the brink of the new era. His message of repentance and his announcement of the end time turn the spotlight on the inauguration of Jesus' messianic ministry. In Mark's Gospel, John also serves as a preview of the fate of Jesus. Just as John is arrested, betrayed and executed, so will be the Son of Man.

Mark begins his story with the advent of John. A biblical quotation attributed to Isaiah but in fact a composite of Exodus 23:20, Malachi 3:1 and Isaiah 40:3, trumpets John's role: he is God's messenger preparing "the way of the Lord"; he is a prophetic voice in the desert calling for the revival of Israel.[2] In short, quick strokes, Mark describes John's ministry. He appears in the *desert* (1:4), a place with profound symbolic meaning in the Bible. In the desert Israel had been created, rescued from slavery in Egypt and forged as a people through the covenant. In the desert, too, Israel had been severely tested, its weakness purified and its commitment deepened.[3] It is not surprising that the Jesus story should begin here with his identity as God's Son revealed (1:11) and the test of his strength undergone (1:12-13).

Mark signals that John's mission is not simply a repeat of other prophetic calls for renewal in Israel's history. John, indeed, preaches repentance (1:4) but the call has a finality

[2] For a discussion of this quotation and its function in the opening verses of Mark's Gospel, cf. R. Guelich, "'The Beginning of the Gospel' Mark 1:1-15," *Biblical Research* 27 (1982), 5-15.

[3] On the symbolism of the desert and its interplay with Mark's presentation of the ministry of John, cf. U. Mauser, *Christ in the Wilderness* (Studies in Biblical Theology 39; Naperville: Allenson, 1963), 77-102, and J. M. Robinson, *The Problem of History in Mark and Other Marcan Studies* (Philadelphia: Fortress, 1982), 72-80.

to it. John's garb of camel's hair and a leather girdle (1:6) is exactly that which identifies Elijah (see II Kings 1:8), the greatest of Israel's prophets and the one expected to return at the beginning of the messianic era. Mark explicitly states this tradition in 9:11 where the disciples ask Jesus, "Why do the scribes say that first Elijah must come?" In his reply Jesus affirms that "Elijah has come, and they did to him whatever they pleased. . ." (9:13). John, in other words, is Elijah *redivivus,*the prophet whose return signaled the New Age.

The massive response to John's preaching seems to reflect the decisive nature of his mission: "and there went out to him *all* the country of Judea and all the people of Jerusalem; and they were baptized by him in the river Jordan, confessing their sins" (1:5). John's own words reveal what Mark has alluded to by swirl of symbol and event. John is the precursor; after him comes the "stronger one," whose sandals John is not worthy to untie. John's ritual of repentance is with water; Jesus will baptize with the Holy Spirit, the gift associated with the Final Age (1:8).

The Baptist's role is, therefore, awesome. He heralds the New Age; he baptizes God's Son; he points to the Messiah. But right from the start Mark begins to unfold the paradoxical nature of the Gospel. John's fate signals that of Jesus: a messenger of God but one who will be humiliated, rejected, even killed in the pursuit of his mission.

The entwined destinies of John and Jesus are alluded to in 1:14, "Now after John had been handed over, Jesus came into Galilee, proclaiming the Gospel of God. . ." This keynote verse enables the evangelist to mark the boundary between John's call for repentance and Jesus' proclamation of the coming rule of God (1:15). But it also links the two figures by subtly tolling Jesus' own fate. Jesus, too, will be "handed over." The Greek verb *paradidomi* is a quasitechnical term within the passion tradition for referring to the arrest of John and Jesus.[4] The passive form of the verb

---

[4] Cf. Mark 1:14; 3:19; 9:31; 10:33; 14:10,11,18,21,41,42,44; 15:1,10,15. Note, too, that the sufferings of the disciples in the pursuit of their mission are described with the same word: cf. 13:9,11.

with its unnamed subject may suggest the divine purpose that flows beneath the destiny of God's messengers. Ultimately, it is God who "hands over" Jesus and his prophetic forebearers. The passion is no absurd tragedy but mysteriously, as some suffering can, effects new life.

The reader of Mark's text is curiously left in the dark about John's fate until chapter 6. The abrupt reference in 1:14 to the arrest carried no details: by whom? for what reason? The information is supplied only in 6:14-29. John's already completed execution is narrated in a flashback (6:16).

The context in which Mark places this story is significant. In 6:1-6 we learn that Jesus encounters opposition and disbelief in "his own country" (6:1). His teaching in the synagogue of Nazareth is not accepted (6:6) and his own people take offense at him, unable to believe that the one who teaches and heals is anyone more than "the carpenter, the son of Mary and brother of James and Joses and Judas and Simon" (6:3). Jesus the prophet is without honor among his own people (6:4).

From this scene of mission and rejection Mark moves to the call of the twelve and their deployment in mission (6:7; cf. the previous call in 3:13-19). They are given power over unclean spirits and are charged to travel light. The tone of the commission is urgent and they are forewarned of opposition and rejection (6:11). The apostles depart and carry out the same mission of proclamation and healing that the Gospel has been attributing to Jesus (6:12-17). In 6:30 we are told of their return and their report to Jesus on what they had done.

It is here, between the sending of the apostles and their return, that Mark places the story about the fate of John. King Herod hears of the impact of the disciples' mission, a mission rooted in the power of Jesus (note that it is Jesus' name that had become known; see Mark 6:14). The identity of Jesus haunts Herod: "Who is this man?" The same probing question is posed by Jesus himself in the crucial scene at Caesarea Philippi. There the popular answers fed back by the disciples are the same as those suggested to Herod:

"John the Baptist," or "Elijah," or "one of the prophets of old" (cf. 8:28 and those recited by "some" in 6:15). Unlike Peter who at least has a glimmer of Jesus' identity (cf. 8:29), Herod erroneously believes that Jesus is "John, whom I beheaded," raised from the dead (6:16). It is at this point that Mark recounts in flashback the macabre tale of John's death (6:17-29). The prophet had been arrested because he had confronted Herod on his unlawful marriage to Herodias, his sister-in-law. Although convinced that John was a just and holy man, and intrigued by John's message, Herod succumbs to his vanity and to the intrigues of Herodias: John is executed unjustly. His disciples come and take the body of their martyred leader for burial.

The reader of the Gospel can easily catch the foreboding parallels between John's fate and that of Jesus. A fearless prophet preaches repentance and is rejected. His opponents plot his death and a reluctant ruler succumbs to their persuasiveness. But ironically even the executioner believes in the ultimate triumph of the prophet: a new prophetic voice is heard and Herod believes that John has been raised from the dead.

Rejection by the ones to whom they were sent was the paradoxical destiny of the prophetic messengers to Israel.[5] So, too, would be the fate of the Son of Man, the "stronger one" to whom the prophets pointed. By stitching this story into the mission of the disciples in chapter 6, Mark seems to allude to the continuation of that destiny in the very mission of those who preach in Jesus' name, a point we will examine below.[6]

Mark returns to the intertwining destinies of John and Jesus for one last time in 11:27-33. The Jewish leaders

5 See, for example, Nehemiah 9:6, "Nevertheless they were disobedient and rebelled against thee and cast they law behind their back and killed thy prophets, who had warned them in order to turn them back to thee, and they committed great blasphemies." On the motif of the rejected prophets, cf. D. Aune, *Prophecy in Early Christianity and the Ancient Mediterranean World* (Grand Rapids: Wm. B. Eerdmans, 1983), 157-59.

6 Cf. below, pp. 37-39.

challenge Jesus, demanding to know by what authority he
had carried out his disruption of the Temple activity (see
11:15-19). Jesus rebuffs their question by asking them about
John: "Was the baptism of John from heaven or from
humans? Answer me"(11:30). The leaders are caught: if they
say from heaven, Jesus will ask them why they did not
believe him; if they say from humans, they may provoke the
people who held John to be a genuine prophet. They choose
to retreat: "we do not know. . ." For Mark the same blindness prevented the leaders from accepting Jesus, one who is
not only a "real prophet" but the Son of God.

The passion of John enables the evangelist to prepare the
reader for the passion of Jesus. John's destiny was that of a
prophet, proclaiming a message of repentance to Israel but
rejected by those who would not listen. The theme of the
rejected prophet points to that mysterious clash between
God's ways and human ways, to that collision between the
impulse for new life and the inability of sinful humanity to
respond to it. But the prophet's fate is not one of unrelieved
gloom. The prophetic word, because it comes from God,
will eventually take root in fertile ground (see Isaiah 55:10-
11) and break out in a harvest of life. Jesus' destiny follows
the pattern of John but the stakes are much higher. Jesus is
more than a prophet; he is the "Stronger One," the son sent
to claim the vineyard (12:6-7). In his dying and rising the
future of the world rests.

II. Plots Against Jesus' Life

Twice during the public ministry of Jesus, Mark reports
plots against his life — vivid reminders to the reader of
Jesus' impending death. In 3:6 we are told, "The Pharisees
went out, and immediately held counsel with the Herodians against him, how to destroy him." Following Jesus'
action in the temple we learn of another plot against him:
"And the chief priests and the scribes heard it (i.e., Jesus'
words against the temple) and sought a way to destroy him;

for they feared him, because all the multitude was astonished at his teaching" (11:18).

By means of these texts Mark clearly signals that the causes of Jesus' death were rooted in the character of his public ministry.

A) THE PLOT IN GALILEE (3:6)

The first plot against Jesus comes early in his Galilean ministry. The Pharisees and Herodians (apparently supporters of the Herodian dynasty) join forces even though historically they would not have been allies. The reasons for their deadly opposition to Jesus are explained in the string of five conflict stories that Mark narrates in the section 2:1 — 3:6.[7] The stories form a discernible unit in the Gospel, with each of them involving a characteristic feature of Jesus' mission as presented by Mark, and each issuing in conflict.

Prior to this section of the Gospel Mark had narrated the explosive and powerful ministry of Jesus as he breaks into Galilee, proclaiming the "Gospel of God" and announcing the advent of God's rule (1:14-15).[8] He calls disciples to follow him and to share in his mission of "fishing for people," a biblical phrase implying the final day of salvation in which Yahweh will snare humanity for judgment (cf. Jeremiah 16:16; Amos 4:2; Habakkuk 1:14-17). The disciples leave their families and livelihood behind and immediately follow Jesus (1:16-20). In rapid succession Mark describes Jesus' liberation of a man with an unclean spirit in the synagogue of Capernaum (1:21-28), the healing of Simon's mother-in-law (1:29-31) and the cure of a leper (1:40-45). Editorial summaries (1:32-34, 45) report that these stories

---

[7] On this section of Mark, cf. J. Dewey, *Markan Public Debate* (SBL Dissertation Series 48; Chico, CA: Scholars Press, 1980). Dewey affirms that Mark has carefully constructed this section of his Gospel to state the directions of Jesus' ministry and the opposition it provoked.

[8] For a broader discussion of the Kingdom motif in the context of Jesus' ministry, cf. W. Kasper, *Jesus the Christ* (New York: Paulist, 1976), 72-88; D. Senior & C. Stuhlmueller, *The Biblical Foundations for Mission* (Maryknoll, NY: Orbis, 1983), 144-60.

are only samples of the overwhelming impact of Jesus'
mission as the power of God's rule makes itself felt.
But beginning in chapter 2 a different type of response
now appears. When Jesus forgives the sins of a paralytic, the
scribes challenge his act: "Why does this man speak thus? It
is blasphemy! Who can forgive sins but God alone?" (2:7).
Jesus calls Levi, the tax collector, to be a disciple and dines
with him and many other tax collectors and sinners. This
association with outcasts scandalizes the scribes, or scholars, of the Pharisee party and they complain to Jesus'
disciples: "Why does he eat with tax collectors and sinners?"
(2:16). When people see that the disciples of John and the
Pharisees fast yet Jesus' disciples do not, they confront him:
"Why do John's disciples and the disciples of the Pharisees
fast, but your disciples do not fast?" (2:18). When Jesus'
disciples seem to violate the sabbath by plucking heads of
grain and eating them as they go through the fields (breaking the law forbidding reaping on the Sabbath, Exodus
34:21), the Pharisees complain to him again, "Look, why are
they doing what is not lawful on the sabbath?" (2:24). The
climax comes in the final story. As the Pharisees silently
watch, ready to accuse Jesus of healing on the sabbath (3:2),
he openly challenges them by commanding the man to
stretch out his hand, restoring it to full health (3:5).

A crucial point is that each of these hostile challenges is
directed to *characteristic* activities of Jesus' mission. The
conflict stories enable Mark to clarify for the reader the
intent and authority of Jesus. The response to each challenge illustrates this. When Jesus is attacked as blasphemous for forgiving the sins of the paralytic, he responds by
affirming that "the Son of Man has authority to forgive
sins" (2:10). The subsequent cure of the paralytic seals both
that authority and the reality of the forgiveness it effects.
For Mark Jesus is the exalted "Son of Man" who will come
in triumph at the end of time (cf. 13:26; 14:62). But already
in Jesus' ministry of compassionate healing that God-given
authority of Jesus is revealed.[9]

[9] On the importance of the "Son of Man" title in Mark's Gospel, cf. below, pp.
29-30.

By inviting Levi, a despised tax collector and one banned
from participation in the religious life of Israel, to become a
disciple — and by celebrating that association in a meal with
other tax collectors and sinners — Jesus proclaims the very
nature of his boundary-breaking mission of compassion:
"those who are well have no need of a physician but those
who are sick; I come not to call the righteous, but sinners"
(2:17). The banquet was a standard symbol of the messianic
hopes of Israel. On Mount Zion, God would spread a lavish
feast where Israel could celebrate in peace and joy (see, for
example, Isaiah 25:6-9). The banquet begun by Jesus throws
open the guest list to repentant sinners, thus challenging the
exclusive norms of his opponents.[10] In connection with the
preceding paralytic story, Mark emphasizes that Jesus' mission was one of forgiveness; it is the lavish and inclusive
proportions of that mission against which Jesus' opponents
protest.

The two Sabbath controversies that conclude the series
(2:23-28 and 3:1-5) continue the sharp focus on Jesus'
authority and the merciful proportions of his mission.
When the Pharisees protest the disciples' plucking the heads
of grain and satisfying their hunger, Jesus reminds them of
David's boldness in using the "bread of the presence" or
sacred loaves put before the Tabernacle on the Sabbath to
feed himself and his companions (Mark's version of the
story is an adaptation of I Samuel 21:1-6). The authority of
Jesus exceeds that of David: ". . .the Son of Man is Lord of
the Sabbath" (2:28). Once again Jesus' interpretation of the
Sabbath law for the sake of human need (2:27) is based on
his God-given authority as Son of Man. In effect, Jesus'
compassion is a disclosure of God's compassion.

The cure of the man with the withered arm moves in the
same direction. Jesus' piercing question is at the heart of the
matter: "Is it lawful on the Sabbath to do good or to do
harm, to save life or kill?" (3:4). Mark portrays the oppo-

10 On the significance of this motif, cf. N. Perrin, *Rediscovering the Teaching of
Jesus* (New York: Harper & Row, 1967), 102-08; E. Schillebeeckx, *Jesus: An
Experiment in Christology* (New York: Seabury, 1979), 206-18.

nents of Jesus as silently hostile; their interpretation of the Sabbath laws has not put concern for human life in first place. Jesus' provocative cure is a wordless rebuttal to such wrong priorities.

The controversy over fasting (2:18-22) stands at the hub of the five conflict stories Mark presents and may provide the interpretive key to all of them. Jesus' disciples do not fast because "the bridegroom is with them" (2:19).[11] That saying is supported by two concluding statements which use different metaphors but make a similar point: a new patch will not hold on old garments (2:21) nor will old wineskins bear new wine (2:22). Each of these sayings affirms that a radical new situation is at hand and the old age must give way and be transformed. Jesus is the bridegroom, the new cloth, the fresh wine. The metaphors point to the authority of Jesus as the Christ, the triumphant Son of Man whose mission ushers in the new age of salvation. The retention of old priorities and resistance to the merciful bounty of his mission are what Mark identifies as the reasons for opposition to Jesus. Conversely, unwavering commitment to the mission of repentance and forgiveness would lead to the cross. The cross, therefore, would be the ultimate expression of Jesus' ministry.

B) THE PLOT IN JERUSALEM (11:18)

The other reference to a plot against Jesus prior to the passion narrative occurs at 11:18. Immediately following Jesus' provocative action in the temple, the chief priests and the scribes "sought a way to destroy him." This threat comes near the culmination of Jesus' ministry and, similar to the conflict of 2:1 — 3:6, Mark uses the occasion to reflect on the ultimate significance of Jesus' mission.

With the triumphant entry into Jerusalem (11:1-10) Mark's story begins a new and decisive chapter. Action will be staged in the Jerusalem temple and its precincts; there

---

[11] For a broader discussion of this passage and the issue of fasting in the New Testament, cf. J. Wimmer, *Fasting in the New Testament: A Study in Biblical Theology* (New York: Paulist, 1982), 85-101.

Jesus will perform a final dramatic sign and engage in a series of conflicts with his opponents (now involving the Jerusalem-based chief priests and Sadducees as well as the scribes and Pharisees) that culminate in his death. The temple is the dominating structure of this section of the story. Mark will use the occasion to assert one of the more intriguing motifs of his theology, one that has direct connection with the passion story.[12] Jesus' opponents mobilize against him because of his actions in the temple (11:15-19). Whatever was the historical reality behind this incident — perhaps a symbolic action on Jesus' part calling for integrity between Israel's worship and its way of life in the manner of the prophets (compare Isaiah 1:12-17) — Mark seems to interpret the action in a far more radical manner than a mere cleansing of the temple. The Marcan Jesus declares the *end* of the temple and the establishment of a new temple "not made by hands" (14:58) and one open to "all nations" (11:17). Evidence of this radical stance can be found throughout chapters 11-12 and, as we will note later, reemerges in the passion narrative itself.[13]

First of all Mark frames the action in the temple with the curious incident of the cursing (11:12-14) and withering (11:20-21) of the fig tree.[14] The fig tree is condemned because it offered no fruit when Jesus was hungry and came looking for figs; its season was out of synchronization with the coming of the Son of Man and so it is condemned. This action-parable becomes a commentary on the fate of the temple itself. Jesus enters the temple to expose its barrenness; the temple commerce is disrupted, and the carrying of the sacred vessels is stopped (11:16). The combined quotations from Isaiah 56:7 and Jeremiah 7:11 toll the temple's

---

[12] On the temple motif in Mark's theology, cf. J. Donahue, *Are You The Christ? The Trial Narrative in the Gospel of Mark* (SBL Dissertation Series 10; Missoula, Montana: Society of Biblical Literature, 1973) and D. Juel, *Messiah and Temple: The Trial of Jesus in the Gospel of Mark* (SBL Dissertation Series 31; Missoula, Montana: Society of Biblical Literature, 1977).

[13] See, below, the discussion of Mark 14:58: 15:29, 38.

[14] This "sandwich" technique is a typical literary device used by Mark to highlight important segments of his story; cf. J. Donahue, *Are You The Christ?*, 42-43.

demise. God's house shall be a house of prayer "for all nations" yet the Jerusalem temple had become a "den of robbers," a phrase used by Jeremiah to condemn the infidelities of Israel. Reverberations continue throughout this section of Mark. The parable of the vineyard (12:1-12) is an allegory on the history of Israel. The vineyard's owner sends messengers to procure the fruits of his vineyard (a traditional symbol of Israel, see Isaiah 5:1-7), but the messengers are rejected, even killed. Finally he sends his Son, but him, too, they murder. For this the tenants are condemned and the vineyard entrusted to others. A quotation from Psalm 118:22-23 connects this story to the temple motif: the rejected stone becomes the cornerstone of a new edifice. This psalm verse is used by I Peter 2:6 and Ephesians 2:20 in referring to the Christian community as the living temple, and it is likely that Mark, too, intends such an allusion. As they did after his action in the temple (11:18), Jesus' opponents react with livid hostility: "And they tried to arrest him, but feared the multitude, for they perceived that he had told the parable against them" (12:12).

Two positive examples augment the temple motif and help clarify its significance for Mark. A scribe quite unlike those who have plotted against Jesus poses a sincere question: "Which commandment is the first of all?" (12:28). Jesus' response, citing love of God and love of neighbor, is admired by the scribe. The man repeats Jesus' answer and adds the conclusion that loving God and neighbor "is much more than all whole burnt offerings and sacrifices" (12:33). Jesus exclaims in praise of the scribe: "You are not far from the kingdom of God!" (12:34). This sense of proportion — the love command as more fundamental than ritual — echoes the sabbath conflicts of 2:23-28 and 3:1-6 and is the key to Mark's radical critique of the temple. It is love that gives meaning to ritual, not the reverse. True worship is guaranteed not by a temple of stone but by a living community of faith.

A similar point is made at the conclusion of chapter 12. The pretentious piety of the scribes masks pride and injustice (12:38-40) and is in total contrast to the widow's minuscule gift of two copper coins (12:41-44). Her gift is worth more than those of the rich because theirs is a fraction of their abundance while she gives "her whole life" (12:44). This poignant scene exposes Mark's basic thought: the widow is a genuine disciple because, like Jesus himself, she gives everything to God. True worship must be just that.

The temple motif thus enables Mark to reflect again on the significance of Jesus' person and ministry. The authority of Jesus is repeatedly asserted in this climactic part of the story. He is the triumphant Messiah who enters the city of David to the acclamation of the crowd (11:8-10). He is the beloved "Son," the last and definitive messenger to Israel (12:6). He is the one whom David had called "Lord" (12:31-37). He is the awesome teacher who stuns his opponents with his wisdom (11:27-33; 12:13-17; 12:18-27; 12:28-34). But above all Jesus is depicted as Lord of the Temple who brings judgment on a temple of stone expressive of the false values of the leaders. Through his death and resurrection he will fashion a community from all nations, whose love of God and neighbor, and whose total commitment of life will make them a living temple.

Mark, therefore, is not describing the actual historical circumstances of the Herodian temple in Jesus' day. Instead he makes the Jerusalem temple a symbol of inauthentic worship, of piety that is hypocritical and exploitive. Such a temple, in Mark's view, is barren and worthy of destruction. We cannot be sure if at the time Mark wrote his Gospel the Jerusalem temple still existed. In 13:2 the destruction of the temple is clearly predicted and it may be that Mark writes his Gospel after AD 70, interpreting the temple's demise as a punishment for the infidelity of Israel and extending this negative symbolism to include the wrong priorities and false piety exemplified by Jesus' opponents in the Gospel story.

In any case the temple motif serves to further elaborate the mortal clash between Jesus and his opponents. His challenge to ritual without love, his insistence on love of God and compassionate love of neighbor as the soul of worship are met with opposition and hostility by those with other priorities. Jesus' assault on the false temple is another impulse toward his death on the cross. Mark will make this connection by the accusation against Jesus at the trial (14:57-58) and by the dramatic event of the tearing of the temple veil at the moment of his death (15:38). At that instant a new worshipping community will be born.

The Galilean and Jerusalem plots are the summit of a wide expanse of opposition against Jesus and his mission in the Gospel. We have considered only some of the conflicts here. The ministry of the Son of Man is no placid triumph; it is wracked with controversy and rejection. The cross is firmly embedded in the provocative character of Jesus' entire life. Jesus proclaims the liberating "Gospel of God" and inaugurates the gracious rule of God. But because that gospel calls for repentance and the realignment of values, because it challenges cherished positions and untouchable assumptions, Jesus is resisted and opposed.

The opposition misreads Jesus; they are blind to his message. Mark reflects on the mystery of this hostility in the parable discourse of chapter 4. Like Jesus himself, the parables become dividing points. For those who are blind and deaf to Jesus' message, the parables are baffling riddles; for those blessed to receive the word, his teaching discloses the mystery of the Kingdom (cf. 4:10-12). But the opposition, no matter how forceful, will not overwhelm God's word. It will fall on good soil and will yield thirty, sixty, a hundred-fold (4:8). Opposition will lead to the cross, but the cross will issue in resurrection.

III. The Way of the Son of Man (8:22-10:52)

Mark prepares his readers for the death of Jesus not only by ominous clashes with the opponents of John and Jesus but also by Jesus' own teaching. Three times in the Gospel Jesus predicts his death and ultimate triumph. These predictions are found in a central part of Mark's narrative and serve as an essential expression of his christology.

Contemporary interpretation of Mark has recognized that a crucial part of the Gospel is to be found in the section beginning with the encounter at Caesarea Philippi (8:27) up to the entrance into Jerusalem (which commences at 11:1).[15] Several structural features set this off as a discrete section of the Gospel.

First of all, the section is punctuated by the three passion and resurrection predictions, where for the first time in the Gospel Jesus openly speaks of his own death. The first (8:31) occurs at Caesarea Philippi immediately after Peter's confession of Jesus as the Christ. The second (9:31) takes place as Jesus and his disciples make their way down through Galilee, from Caesarea Philippi to Capernaum. The third (10:33-34) as they move toward Jerusalem.

In each prediction the title used by Jesus is the "Son of Man." It is the "Son of Man" who is to "suffer much," "be rejected," "be killed," etc. This mysterious title is an important part of Mark's theology. Although the origin and use of the title in early Christianity is much debated, it is clear that for Mark it becomes a touchstone for properly understanding Jesus.[16] The Risen Christ is identified with the apocalyptic Son of Man (see Daniel 7:14) who will come in triumph at the parousia (Mark 13:26; 14:62). Through the powerful deeds of his ministry Jesus is also depicted as exercising the power of the Son of Man on earth (2:10, 28). But, above all, Jesus is the Son of Man in his experience of suffering and death (8:31; 9:31; 10:33). The vague content of the Son of Man title may have enabled Mark to appropriate it to this specific usage. To confess Jesus as Son of Man was to recognize that his way was the way of service, of giving life for others (10:45). All other titles applied to Jesus such as

[15] See, for example, N. Perrin, "The Interpretation of the Gospel of Mark," *Interpretation* 30 (1976), 115-24; E. Best, *Following Jesus: Discipleship in the Gospel of Mark* (Journal For The Study of the New Testament, Supplement Series 4; Sheffield: University of Sheffield, 1981), 15-18.

[16] On the use of this title in Mark, cf. N. Perrin, *A Modern Pilgrimage in New Testament Christology* (Philadelphia: Fortress, 1974), 84-93; for further background on the possible origin of the title, cf. J. Dunn, *Christology in the Making* (Philadelphia: Westminster, 1980), 65-97.

"Son of God" or "Messiah" were capable of carrying the wrong connotations. Only if these were used in conjunction with the Son of Man designation could the proper confession of Jesus' identity be assured. When Peter confesses Jesus as the "Christ" or Messiah (8:29), Jesus responds by beginning to teach the disciples that the "*Son of Man* must suffer many things..." (8:31). Peter's subsequent attempt to silence Jesus shows that, indeed, his conception of the "Christ" was not yet ready to accommodate the notion of a suffering Son of Man.

A) THE JOURNEY

The placement of the predictions suggests that Mark casts this whole section into the format of a "journey" from Galilee to Jerusalem.[17] It is "on the way" (8:27) that Jesus confronts the disciples with the decisive question of the entire Gospel: "Who do you say that I am?" (8:29). As they move down through Galilee towards Capernaum Jesus asked the disciples what they were discussing "on the way" (9:33, 34). In 10:1 and 10:17 the progress of the journey "through" Judea and beyond the Jordan is noted. It is most dramatically stated in 10:32, introducing the final passion prediction: "And they were on the way, going up to Jerusalem and Jesus was walking ahead of them; and they were amazed, and those who followed were afraid. And taking the twelve again, he began to tell them what was to happen to him saying, "Behold we are going up to Jerusalem..." The final scene of the section — the cure of a blind man at Jericho — is introduced and concluded with reference to the journey. As Jesus passes through Jericho he sees Bartimaeus sitting "alongside the way" (10:46). After receiving his sight, Bartimaeus follows Jesus "on the way" (10:52).

As we shall see, the scope of the journey is far wider than the few kilometers from Galilee to Jerusalem. Mark will use the journey as a basic theological symbol.

17 For a discussion of the journey motif in Mark, cf. W. Kelber, *The Kingdom in Mark: A New Place and a New Time* (Philadelphia: Fortress, 1976), 67-85; E. Manicardi, *Il cammino di Gesù nel Vangelo di Marco. Schema narrativo e tema cristologico* (Analecta Biblica 96; Rome: Biblical Institute Press, 1981).

B) THE DISCIPLES

Another striking feature of this section is the reaction of the disciples: after each of the passion predictions they seem to grossly misunderstand Jesus.[18] At Caesarea Philippi Peter attempts to silence Jesus' prediction of death (8:31). The counter reaction of Jesus is directed to all the disciples as well as to Peter (note the phrase "eyeing the disciples, he rebuked Peter" in 8:33): "Get behind me, Satan! For you are not thinking according to the ways of God but in a human way." This extraordinary rebuke reveals the depth of Peter's misunderstanding and suggests that his previous confession of Jesus as the "Christ" was defective (8:29). After the second Passion prediction, Jesus' question to the disciples — "What were you discussing on the journey?" (9:33) — again illustrates that they are out of synchronization with Jesus. They fall silent because "on the journey, they had been disputing about which of them was the greatest" (9:34), a stark contrast with Jesus' own declaration about his impending humiliation and death. A similar jarring dispute between the disciples' own viewpoint and that of Jesus follows the third passion prediction. Jesus' statement about his death is immediately followed by the sons of Zebedee asking for positions of power at Jesus' right and left hand (10:37). The rest of the disciples share in this blatant failure when they become indignant at the nimble maneuver of James and John (10:41).

In each instance, Jesus' prediction of suffering and giving of life is met by resistance or by attitudes of crass arrogance and ambition. There are other incidents in this section which show the disciples in a similar light. Their lack of faith prevents them from exorcising the possessed boy (9:14-29). They attempt to stop a man, not of their company, who was casting out demons in Jesus' name, earning a rebuke from Jesus for such exclusiveness (9:38-41). And they attempt to

---

[18] The role of the disciples in Mark has become a major focal point for contemporary interpretation of the Gospel. See, for example, E. Best, *Following Jesus*; R. C. Tannehill, "The Disciples in Mark: The Function of a Narrative Role," *Journal of Religion* 57 (1977), 386-405; A. Stock, *Call to Discipleship: A Literary Study of Mark's Gospel* (Good News Studies 1; Wilmington: Michael Glazier, Inc., 1982).

prevent the children from coming to Jesus, drawing his anger (10:13-16).

The two stories of cures of blindness which flank this section of the Gospel may serve as Mark's commentary on the plight of the disciples. Right before the scene at Caesarea Philippi and the start of the journey section, Jesus cures a blind man at Bethsaida. It is a case of deep-seated blindness and, curiosly, Jesus must repeat his efforts to restore the man to full sight (8:22-26). At the conclusion of the journey, as Jesus leaves Jericho on the way to Jerusalem, he encounters another blind man, Bartimaeus (10:46-52). Mark presents this entire encounter as a call to discipleship.[19] While those around Jesus (possibly the disciples, cf. 10:46-48) attempt to stifle the blind man's cries for mercy, Jesus hears his plea and calls the man to himself. His desire "to see" is interpreted by Jesus as deep faith which not only restores the man's sight but makes him a disciple (10:52).

Both stories together make an apt frame for the whole journey section and highlight the issue of discipleship. The disciples are afflicted with deep-seated spiritual blindness, unable to grasp the identity of Jesus and the impact of his mission. Only faith and the healing power of Jesus can restore their sight and confirm their call to discipleship.

Note that each display of misunderstanding by the disciples prompts Jesus to instruct them on the meaning of genuine discipleship. Here is another important function of the journey narrative in Mark. Jesus responds to Peter's misunderstanding by gathering the disciples and the crowd together and instructing them:

> [34]..."If any one would come after me, let him deny himself and take up his cross and follow me. [35]For whoever would save his life will lose it; and whoever loses his life for my sake and the gospel's will save it. [36]For what does it

[19] Cf. P. Achtemeier, "'And he followed him'; Miracles and Discipleship in Mark 10:46-52," *Semeia* 11 (1978), 115-45; also, E. Johnson, "Mark 10:46-52: Blind Bartimaeus," *Catholic Biblical Quarterly* 40 (1978), 191-204; V. K. Robbins, "The Healing of Blind Bartimaeus (10:46-52) in the Marcan Theology," *Journal of Biblical Theology* 92 (1973), 224-43.

profit anyone to gain the whole world and forfeit their life? [37]For what can someone give in return for his life?" (8:34-37).

Note that the instruction uses the language of the cross and the giving of life as metaphors for genuine discipleship.

The same pattern emerges after the second passion prediction. The disciples' shamed silence over their argument about greatness is followed by Jesus' teaching, "If any one would be first, they must be last of all and servant of all" (9:35). The last passion prediction and the corresponding misunderstanding on the part of James and John lead to one of the most important discipleship instructions in the entire Gospel. Their request for places of power is countered by Jesus' question: "You do not know what you are asking. Are you able to drink the cup that I drink, or to be baptized with the baptism with which I am baptized?" (10:38). These allusions to sharing in Jesus' death are amplified for all of the disciples in 10:42-45:

> [42]And Jesus called them to him and said to them, "You know that those who are supposed to rule over the Gentiles lord it over them, and their great ones exercise authority over them. [43]But it shall not be so among you; but whoever would be great among you must be your servant [44]and whoever would be first among you must be slave of all. [45]For the Son of man also came not to be served but to serve, and to give his life as a ransom for many."

The Son of Man's giving of life in ransom for the many is an act of service (see also 9:35) that contrasts sharply with the exploitive use of power and authority that characterizes the "great ones" of the Gentiles who "lord it over" those they rule. Greatness for the disciples consists in giving of life not in snatching it or exploiting it. The interpretation of Jesus' death as an act of service is a loadstone of Mark's theology.

The instructions on discipleship which follow each passion prediction point to a trademark of this entire section of the Gospel. From the beginning of Jesus' ministry up to

Caesarea Philippi (1:14-8:27), Mark's narrative is dominated by the powerful deeds of Jesus. This segment of the gospel takes place mainly in Galilee and illustrates the explosive exorcisms and healings of Jesus who proclaims the Gospel of God, liberating humanity from the grip of evil and inaugurating God's rule. But in the journey section (8:22-10:52) the mood radically shifts. For the first time Jesus speaks of his death and the reader's attention is turned toward Jerusalem and the foreboding events to take place there. Jesus' miracle working activity seems to shut down. Except for the two stories of the blind man which serve as a frame for the journey (cf. above) and the exorcism of the young boy (which really serves to illustrate the disciples' failure, cf. 9:14-29) no further miracles are narrated. The mid-section of the gospel is dominated by teaching, with the spotlight focused almost exclusively on Jesus and his disciples. It is in this section of the gospel that the "hard sayings" of the Gospel are found: the call to lose one's life (8:35), to become like a child (9:35), to put aside possessions and family for the sake of the Gospel (10:17-31), to serve rather than be served (10:45).

On the other side of the journey narrative is Jerusalem. Beginning with chapter 11 Jesus enters the Holy City where conflicts erupt with the Jewish leaders. And, after the discourse on the Mount of Olives in chapter 13, this final third of the gospel will be dominated by the passion narrative (14-15) and the discovery of the empty tomb (16:1-8).

Thus Mark's narrative falls into three major sections, with the magnetic force of the cross the decisive ongoing principle of division. The bountiful mission in Galilee (1:14-8:21) contrasts with the conflict and death that dominate the events in Jerusalem (11:1-16:8). Galilee therefore has basically a positive value in Mark while Jerusalem has a mainly negative one.[20] Mark even tags some of the opponents who appear in the Galilee section of the

[20] Cf. J. M. VanCangh, "La Galilée dans l'évangile de Marc: un lieu theologique?" *Revue Biblique* 79 (1972), 59-75; E. Malbon, "Galilee and Jerusalem: History and Literature in Marcan Interpretation," *The Catholic Biblical Quarterly* 44 (1982), 242-55.

gospel as being "from Jerusalem" (3:22; 7:1). Galilee, by contrast, is the place of mission, the place where the Kingdom erupts (1:14, 28, 39), where disciples are called (1:16-20; 2:14) and where Jew and Gentile experience the Gospel (note the mission journey that begins in 4:24). Not surprisingly it is to "Galilee" that the disciples will be sent to encounter the risen Christ at the conclusion of the gospel (cf. 14:28; 16:7).[21] The journey section (8:22-10:52) binds together these two polarities of the narrative. The disciples are invited to follow Jesus in his way from Galilee to Jerusalem. In the crucible of death the ultimate nature of his mission and the proof of genuine discipleship will be revealed.

The various elements we have sketched indicate that the journey section of Mark is, indeed, an important preparation for the passion of Jesus. The focus of the story dramatically shifts from the Galilean ministry of Jesus to the foreboding events of Jerusalem. The fate of John the Baptist and the plot of the opponents against Jesus had already tolled the death bell, but now, for the first time, the passion is spoken of openly by Jesus himself and the reader is moved inexorably towards the climactic events of the cross.

C) THE CROSS AS REVELATION AND CRISIS

Mark also uses the journey motif to show how the cross is central to his christology. The opening scenes of the Gospel had made powerful assertions about Jesus: the title verse (1:1) had proclaimed him as the "Christ, the Son of God." John as Elijah returned had affirmed that Jesus was the "Stronger One," the one who would baptize with the Spirit of the messianic age (1:6-8). At the moment of baptism the Spirit of God descended on Jesus and the heavenly voice declared him as God's Son (1:10-11). And in the desert, Jesus had proved himself as the messianic liberator, defeating the power of Satan, a preview of the ultimate outcome of his ministry (1:12-13).

Throughout Jesus' Galilean ministry his messianic power was displayed in vivid fashion through healing, exorcism,

---

[21] See the discussion of these key texts, below pp. 136-137.

and authoritative teaching. The demons acclaim him as "Son of God" (5:7; see also 1:24). But curiously Jesus' identity seems muted for the characters in the Gospel. His opponents assert that he is in league with Satan (3:22). His family thinks he is insane (3:21) and his own village reacts in disbelief to "Mary's son" (6:3). The disciples, too, seem obtuse, unable to decipher Jesus' parables (4:10), baffled by his identity (4:41; 6:52) and the significance of his ministry (8:17-21). They share in the same blindness that seems to grip Jesus' opponents (compare 8:17-18 with 4:12).

This hidden, muted aspect of Jesus' Galilean ministry helps direct the reader forward in the Gospel. The full story of Jesus is not told in the powerful deeds of Galilee. The spirit of that ministry could be ambiguous; the opponents, for example, judge that it is done in league with Beelzebul (3:22). For Mark the touchstone of authenticity will be the cross. The spirit of Jesus' ministry of healing and exorcism is not exploitive, nor is it a raw display of power for the sake of aggrandizement. It is an act of love, an act of service on behalf of the many. The Son of Man's total giving of life — his death on behalf of others — is the authenticating force behind his entire mission (cf. 10:45).

Therefore, the disciples, too, must be willing to walk from Galilee to Jerusalem with Jesus. Unless they could absorb the message of the cross their fascination with the power of Jesus would be counterfeit. Mark's portrayal of the disciples is one of the most fascinating features of his Gospel. Rather than idealize the first followers of Jesus, Mark seems to highlight their weakness and failure. In the early chapters of the Gospel they often appear confused and baffled; in the journey section they misunderstand Jesus and recoil before the message of the cross. And, as we shall see, in the passion story itself they abjectly fail. In the body of his Gospel, therefore, Mark alerts us to the cross as a crisis for discipleship. Unless the follower of Jesus is willing to give his or her life to others, discipleship will run aground on the shoals of arrogance and exploitation. The passion, therefore, is both the ultimate revelation of Jesus' identity and the ultimate test for the disciples.

IV. The Passion of the Community

In the body of his Gospel Mark alerts the reader to another dimension of the passion, one closely linked to the motifs we have already considered. The Gospel forewarns the reader that not only will Jesus be rejected and killed, so too, will the community that lives in his name. This "passion of the community" is hinted at in chapter 6 when Mark embeds the story of John's execution by Herod in the account of the disciples' mission (6:7-13, 14-29, 30-31). As Jesus sends out his disciples to take up his own mission of liberating humanity from evil (6:7, 13) they are warned: "if any place will not receive you and they refuse to hear you, when you leave, shake off the dust that is on your feet for a testimony against them" (6:11). The discipleship instructions during the journey to Jerusalem speak pointedly of "taking up the cross" (8:34), of "losing one's life" (8:35), of "drinking the cup" and "being baptized" with the same cup of pain and immersion in death as Jesus (10:39). In 10:30 "persecutions" are ironically included in the list of rewards for following Jesus.

But it is especially in chapter 13, the so-called "apocalyptic discourse," that the connection between the passion of Jesus and the passion of the community is made.[22] As he sits with his disciples on the Mount of Olives, overlooking the stunning scene of Jerusalem and its temple, Jesus speaks of the temple's coming destruction and of the travails the community will experience as it moves out in history toward the consummation of the world. Rather than speculating about the timing of the end, the discourse discourages such

[22] This chapter is important for deciphering Mark's theology and the situation of his community. Although many interpreters believe that Mark's church lived in imminent expectation of the parousia, there are suggestions in the discourse of chapter 13 that Mark foresaw an extended period before the final day. Rather than building up apocalyptic expectations about the endtime, the discourse seems ultimately to discourage them. On this cf. C. Cousar, "Eschatology and Mark's Theologia Crucis. A Critical Analysis of Mark 13," *Interpretation* 24 (1970), 321-35; also, D. Senior & C. Stuhlmueller, *The Biblical Foundations for Mission*, 220-21.

thinking. Those who alarm the community about an imminent end are branded "false prophets" (13:5-6, 21-22). The end will come only after the Gospel has been proclaimed to the whole world (13:10). Then the triumphant Son of Man will gather his chosen ones from the four winds and from the ends of the earth to the ends of heaven (13:26-27), a beautiful image of human destiny as a world-wide community. But no one except God knows the time — not even the Son (13:32).

Instead of speculating on the time of the final day, the disciples are urged to be alert and to commit themselves fully to their world-wide mission (13:10). This is the core of the discourse and it is here (13:9-13) that warnings erupt about the sufferings involved in proclaiming the Gospel. The disciples will be "delivered up to councils," "beaten in synagogues," and called to give testimony before "governors and kings" (13:9). They will be tried and "delivered up" (13:11). There will be divisions among households and even betrayal by family members as "brother will deliver up brother to death, and the father his child, and children will rise against parents and have them put to death" (13:12). The disciples will be "hated by all for my name's sake" (13:13).

Mark describes the suffering to be endured by the community in the pursuit of its mission in terms evocative of Jesus' own rejection, trial and death. The word used for "deliver up" (13:9, 11, 12) is *paradidomi*, the quasi-technical word used repeatedly in the Gospel to describe Jesus' own deliverance to death.[23] Just as Jesus encountered opposition, rejection and ultimately death in his commitment to proclaim the "Gospel of God," so will the community if it is committed to proclaim the gospel to all nations in Jesus' name (13:10). Once again Mark makes a direct connection between the mission of Jesus and the cross.

The position of the final discourse immediately before the passion narrative helps it serve as an important orientation to the reader. The story of suffering, death and yet ultimate

23 Cf. above, p. 17, n.4.

triumph that is about to unfold, is not simply a story from the past, nor only a story about the fate of Jesus. It is now the story of the community's own struggle with death. Mark puts this connection in relief by the way he concludes the discourse. The community is warned to "stay awake," that is, to adopt a stance of watchfulness like the sentry on the perimeter of the camp, alert to any hint of crisis when action must be taken (see the images of 13:33-37). The Christian is to be awake, watching for those moments of opportunity when God's grace breaks into history.

Mark deftly ties this motif into the passion story. In 13:35 the watches of the night are ticked off: evening, midnight, cockcrow, morning. These identical moments of time will be noted in the passion story itself, as it progresses from the Last Supper to the trial before Pilate: evening (14:17), night (14:30), cockcrow (14:72), dawn (15:1). In the course of this nighttime Jesus is alert, watching and praying as his crisis approaches (cf. 14:34,38). But the disciples "sleep" and are tragically unprepared (14:37,40,41). The passion of Jesus is also the passion of the community.

Conclusion

Mark, then, carefully prepares the reader for the climax of the Gospel story. Jesus' arrest and death, despite their scandalous and dramatic tones, are no surprise. The Marcan Jesus moves unerringly toward the cross, a cross that is both the full expression of his mission of giving life to all in need and the gauge of how deeply the Gospel clashes with the values and assumptions of the world.

PART II

THE PASSION
(Mark 14:1-15:47)

Introduction

We are now ready to read closely Mark's passion story. The extensive scope of this narrative and its singular focus on the last hours of Jesus' life make it a unique section of the Gospel. As we have already suggested Mark depends on a pre-existing narrative for much of this material, but has thoroughly recast it to express his own style and theological perspective.[1]

Our goal here is not to consider the vast historical issues surrounding the arrest, trial and death of Jesus.[2] Instead we will accept the account Mark has presented to us, lingering over the brush strokes in his bold portrayal of Jesus' passion and attempting to catch the message of his story.

[1] Cf. above, pp. 9-11.

[2] On the historical background of the passion, see E. Bammel (ed.), *The Trial of Jesus* (Studies in Biblical Theology 10; London: SCM, 1970); J. Blinzler, *The Trial of Jesus* (Westminster, MD: Newman, 1958); D. R. Catchpole, *The Trial of Jesus: A Study in the Gospels and Jewish Historiography from 1770 to the Present Day* (Leiden: Brill, 1971); E. Lohse, *History of the Suffering and Death of Jesus Christs* (Philadelphia: Fortress, 1967); G. S. Sloyan, *Jesus on Trial. The Development of the Passion Narratives and Their Historical and Ecumenical Implications* (Philadelphia: Fortress, 1973); W. R. Wilson, *The Execution of Jesus. A Judicial, Literary and Historical Investigation* (New York: Scribners, 1970).

Mark's passion narrative is fast paced and taut, beginning with a prelude (14:1-10) in which the plot against Jesus' life is renewed, moving through the Last Supper (14:12-31), the events in Gethsemane (14:32-52), the trial before the High Priest (14:53-72) and Pilate (15:1-20), and finally crucifixion (15:21-41) and burial (15:42-47). We will examine each scene in turn.

I. Fidelity and Betrayal:
The Passion Begins (14:1-10)

Mark begins the passion story abruptly with three scenes presented in jolting contrast to each other. The reports of the death plot by the leaders (14:1-2) and Judas' betrayal (14:10-11) envelop an anonymous woman's act of tenderness like soiled paper around a jewel.[3] The three scenes rekindle the themes of christology and discipleship that dominate Mark's Gospel, particularly in his reflection on the cross.

14 It was two days before the Passover and the Feast of Unleavened Bread. And the chief priests and the scribes were seeking how to arrest him by stealth, and kill him; [2]for they said, "Not during the feast, lest there be a tumult of the people."

[3]And while he was at Bethany in the house of Simon the leper, as he sat at table, a woman came with an alabaster flask of ointment of pure nard, very costly, and she broke the flask and poured it over his head. [4]But there were some who said to themselves indignantly, "Why was the ointment thus wasted? [5]For this ointment might have been sold for more than three hundred denarii, and given to the poor." And they reproached her. [6]But Jesus said, "Let her alone; why do you trouble her? She has done a beautiful thing to me. [7]For you always have the poor with you, and whenever you will, you can do good to them; but

---

[3] This is another instance of Mark's technique of intercalation or framing of an important scene; cf. J. Donahue, *Are You the Christ?*, 60.

you will not always have me. [8]She has done what she could; she has anointed my body beforehand for burying. [9]And truly, I say to you, wherever the gospel is preached in the whole world, what she has done will be told in memory of her." [10]Then Judas Iscariot, who was one of the twelve, went to the chief priests in order to betray him to them. [11]And when they heard it they were glad, and promised to give him money. And he sought an opportunity to betray him. (14:1-11)

A) TIME FOR THE PLOT (14:1-2)

Instead of a formal introduction to the passion story, Mark shifts the reader with stunning rapidity from the cosmic vision of the apocalyptic discourse to the chilling tones of the plot against Jesus.[4] The last word of the discourse on the Mount of Olives had been: "What I say to you I say to all: Stay awake" (13:37). Now the reason for watching is clear: the crisis is at hand.

Mark states the time: "two days before the Passover and the feast of Unleavened Bread" (14:1). The chronology is somewhat murky. The Jewish feast of Passover took place on the 15th day of the month of Nisan, the day formerly beginning with sundown the evening before (the 14th) according to the usual Jewish calculation. The Feast of Unleavened Bread was originally a separate festival time, beginning on Passover and lasting a week until the twenty-first day of Nisan. By the first century the two feasts were referred to in combination (cf. II Chronicles 35:17; also in Josephus). The term "two days before" probably is to be taken in the Jewish sense of *the day before*, thereby placing the plot and anointing on Wednesday, the day before the Thursday evening on which the Passover feast would be inaugurated and when Jesus would celebrate the Passover meal with his disciples (14:12).

---

[4] Matthew (26:1-2) will alter Mark here to begin the passion with a more formal introduction. Mark uses a Greek connective *de* ("but") which ties 14:1 to the ending of chapter 13. On the apocalyptic discourse, cf. above, pp. 37-39.

However Mark is less than precise in all this. In 14:12 he identifies the "First day of Unleavened Bread" (=Passover) as the day on which the Passover lamb was sacrificed. In fact the lambs for the meal were slaughtered in the afternoon. The feast formally began only in the evening. By "first day" here he seems to use a midnight to midnight time division (as was the Hellenistic custom) and, therefore, to mean Thursday.

It is unlikely that Mark intends to be scrupulously accurate about the dating of the feast. The basic chronology serves his dramatic purpose. Jesus will die on the Passover, that is, Friday (note that burial must be hastened since the eve of the Sabbath loomed, 15:42). He will celebrate the Passover meal with his disciples on Thursday night (14:12). On the day before these momentous events — Wednesday — the plot against his life is triggered.

The plot against Jesus sprung in the wake of his temple action will now bear fruit. But Jesus' majesty is still in play; the leaders fear his impact on the crowds, as Mark noted before (11:18; 12:12). And even though their plot will be successful, they are not fully in control. They decide *not* to arrest Jesus "during the feast" but the destiny of the Son of Man will be otherwise. He *will* give his life for the many on the day of Israel's liberation feast.

B) THE BURIAL ANOINTING (14:3-9)

The anointing story contrasts sharply with the furtive plot of the leaders. Jesus returns to Bethany, his place of lodging while at Jerusalem (cf. 11:11-12). Unlike John who reports Jesus' friendship with Mary and Martha and Lazarus at Bethany, Mark provides no details on Jesus' connection to this village over the brow of the Mount of Olives.[5] The story is abruptly introduced. He dines at the home of "Simon the

---

[5] John 11:1-44 places Mary, Martha and Lazarus at Bethany. Luke 10:38-42 mentions Jesus' friendship with Mary and Martha but does not mention Lazarus or the location of the village where they live. Note that Luke's version of the anointing story is not connected with the passion narrative and is quite different from that of Mark; compare Luke 7:36-50.

Leper" (14:3). Again no details are given. Jesus cured a leper in Galilee (1:40-45) but there is no suggestion that he was Simon. By dining with a leper (we do not know if he had been cured or still bore the disease), Jesus continues his association with outcasts (cf. 2:16-17) but Mark does not stress that point here. The spotlight falls instead on the splendid action of the woman and Jesus' vigorous defense of her.

The woman approaches, breaks open an alabaster flask of nard oil (an expensive ointment made from the roots of a rare Indian plant) and anoints Jesus' head. Kings were inaugurated by anointing their head with oil. Although the symbolism of Jesus' messianic dignity may be implied here, it will be submerged by Jesus' interpretation of the act as a *burial* anointing.[6]

The woman's gracious gesture is challenged by some of those present (14:4). In Matthew these "some" are identified as the disciples (Mt 26:8) and in John as Judas Iscariot (John 12:4). Though Mark usually highlights the disciples' obtuseness, he does not take the opportunity here. The bystanders protest the "waste" of such expensive oil. It was worth three hundred denarii which some scholars calculate as the year's wages of an ordinary laborer. The ointment could have been sold and the proceeds given to the poor. Almsgiving was a sacred obligation, particularly in the Passover season.[7]

Jesus' defense of the woman is vigorous and demonstrates how this story fits into Mark's interpretation of Jesus' death. First of all, Jesus contradicts the judgment of her critics. In anointing him the woman has done "a beautiful deed" (v.6) She has not given alms but has done something equally valuable in Jewish piety — she has performed a personal work of love for one in need. But there is more: she has seized the opportunity and done this act of love *to Jesus*. It is here that Mark's perspective emerges. The woman has

---

[6] The Kingship of Jesus will become a major motif of Mark's passion story, especially in the Roman trial; cf. below, pp. 108-114.

[7] Cf. R. Pesch, *Das Markusevangelium*. (Herder theologischer Kommentar zum Neuen Testament; Freiburg/Basel/Wien: Herder, 1980) II, 332.

recognized that Jesus is destined for death and she has offered her precious gift to him.

This is the meaning of verse 7, a verse whose significance has been so frequently distorted in Christian interpretation: "For you always have the poor with you, and whenever you will, you can do good to them; but you will not always have me." Jesus' words are not a prediction of the inevitability of poverty but a disclosure of the woman's insight in anointing Jesus. They will *not always have Jesus*: he is on the brink of death. "Timing" is an important feature of Mark's Gospel. Jesus had defended his disciples for not fasting because one should not fast when the bridegroom is present (cf. 2:19). There would come a time when he is taken away, then fasting would be called for (2:20). Likewise, the fig tree was condemned and withered because it was not ready when Jesus came to it for fruit (11:12-24). The disciples were warned in the final discourse: "Watch, therefore, . . . lest he come suddenly and find you asleep" (13:34-35).

The woman is defended because she alone has sensed the "time." She performs a beautiful act of love and generosity for Jesus, the "poorest of the poor."[8] "She has done what she could," Jesus says. The words are reminiscent of Jesus' praise for another nameless woman, the widow, who puts her whole living into the temple treasury (compare 14:8 and 12:44). Jesus contrasted the widow's total commitment with the pretentious piety of the scribes (12:38-40) and the painless gifts of the rich (12:41-44). She was a true disciple, as is the woman at Bethany.

A further reason for defending the woman is brought forward in v.8b: "she has anointed my body beforehand for burying." Because of the rapid approach of the Sabbath after Jesus' death, there would be no time for the customary anointing of his body (cf. below, 15:42-47. The women would come after the Sabbath to attempt it, 16:1). The anointing takes place now, before Jesus dies. Mark thus ties the anointing story firmly into the passion narrative. What could have been a typical example of Jesus' conflicts with

8 R. Pesch, *Das Markusevangelium* II, 333.

his opponents in the course of his ministry is now an event pointing directly to his death. The scene highlights Jesus' prophetic knowledge of his impending death (in contrast to the furtive miscalculations of his opponents, cf. 14:1-2) as well as the genuine discipleship of a woman who recognizes that Jesus' way will lead to the cross.[9]

The final verse (14:4) shows the importance of this scene for Mark's theology: "Amen I say to you, wherever the gospel is preached in the whole world, what she has done will be told in memory of her." The woman's recognition of Jesus' approaching death and her graceful and lavishly generous response define authentic discipleship for Mark. The women who stand at the cross (15:40-41) are similarly characterized; they have come with Jesus from Galilee to the cross itself (unlike the other disciples who have fled) and they "ministered" to him. The term *diakonein*, "to serve," does not imply mere domestic service in Jesus' behalf but is a quasi-technical word for Christian ministry in the world. Jesus himself is the *diakonos* or servant who gives his life for the many (10:45). In the final discourse Jesus had instructed the community to continue with its preaching of the Gospel "to all nations" (13:10). Here the global sense of the mission is put in even more striking terms — *eis holon ton kosmon* —"to the whole world" (14:9). Wherever the Gospel is preached her story will be told because this story *is* Gospel, the "Good News" of Jesus' liberating death and the call to respond to it.

Thus at the very beginning of the passion story, as opposition and treachery mount against Jesus, Mark lifts up an example of authentic discipleship. Not one of the twelve but a woman, whom the tradition has not even graced with a name, one shunted aside in a patriarchal culture, becomes the paradigm. She takes her place alongside other such

---

[9] On the role of women as types of discipleship in Mark, cf. M. Selvidge, "'And Those Who Followed Feared' (Mark 10:32)," *Catholic Biblical Quarterly* 45 (1983), 396-400; A. Stock, *Call to Discipleship*, 179-80; D. Rhoads & D. Michie, *Mark as Story: An Introduction to the Narrative of a Gospel* (Philadelphia: Fortress, 1982), 129-36. Rhoads and Michie characterize the women as part of a cast of "little people" whose positive responses to Jesus serve as "foils" to the disciples' failures.

provocative examples in the Gospel: Levi (2:14), the Gadarene demoniac (5:1-20), the Syro-Phoenician woman (7:24-30), Bartimaeus, the blind beggar (10:46-52), the widow (12:41-44), the Centurion (15:39), Joseph of Arimathea (15:42-47). Each is a paradoxical reminder to the community that "outsiders" often respond with far greater insight and generosity than the "insiders" oblivious to the presence of grace.

C) JUDAS' BETRAYAL (14:10-11)

Mark wrenches the attention of the reader from a scene of authentic discipleship to one of abject discipleship failure: "Judas Iscariot, one of the Twelve" leaves Jesus' company and goes to his enemies, the priests. Mark had named Judas in the list of the Twelve at their first appointment and had already designated him as the betrayer (3:19). We may presume that Judas' departure (14:10) was from Bethany since Mark had explicitly noted the Twelve's presence with Jesus there in 11:11. Thus it was from a scene of poignant devotion to Jesus that the betrayer leaves for an act of treachery. He goes to the priests who in 11:18 (also 12:12) and 14:1-2 were prominent among those seeking a chance to arrest and kill Jesus.

The chief priests are happy when they hear Judas' offer; now their fears of Jesus (11:18) and of the crowds he attracted (12:12; 14:2) can be overcome. They promise to give Judas money. Unlike Matthew (26:15) and John (12:6), Mark does not suggest that avarice was Judas' motivation; in fact no reason at all is given for the betrayal. Judas is the negative exponent of discipleship; his role is one-dimensional and tragic. His purpose is to "deliver up" Jesus. The word used in verses 10 and 11 for "betray" is *paradidimi,* the recurring word for the moment of Jesus' handing over to his enemies.[10] In most instances, as in the passion predictions, it occurs in the passive voice, subtly implying that Jesus is delivered up ultimately by *God's* design. Judas has his own dark purpose but unwittingly he is part of a

[10] Cf. above, p. 17, n.4.

cosmic drama in which he will be merely an instrument. This point will be made in 14:21 when Jesus states: "The Son of Man goes as it is written of him but woe to that man by whom the Son of Man is betrayed."

More will be said about Judas in the supper scene (see 14:17-21) where the note of broken friendship will be elaborated. But at this point in the drama Mark has brought on stage most of his main cast. Only the Romans are yet to be introduced. The backdrop of the approaching Passover feast has been illumined and the final plot against Jesus picks up momentum. A woman's act of compassion reveals that Jesus is well aware of his approaching death so that the furtive collusion of his enemies and his betrayer will not take him by surprise. The reader is now ready for the drama to unfold as Judas and his allies seek an opportune moment to seize Jesus (14:11).

II. The Final Passover (14:12-31)

The next series of scenes cluster around the final meal of Jesus and his disciples. The disciples are dispatched to prepare the Passover (14:12-16). The solemn and theologically rich moment of the meal (14:22-25) is surrounded by two scenes where discipleship failure is again Mark's poignant theme: Jesus predicts the betrayal of Judas (14:17-21), the denial of Peter and the flight of all the rest (14:26-31). The institution account with its stress on the deep bond between Jesus and his followers and Jesus' ultimate triumph over death is a strong counterpoint to the surrounding scenes which brood over discipleship weakness and failure.

12And on the first day of Unleavened Bread, when they sacrificed the passover lamb, his disciples said to him, "Where will you have us go and prepare for you to eat the passover?" 13And he sent two of his disciples, and said to them, "Go into the city, and a man carrying a jar of water will meet you; follow him, 14and wherever he enters, say to the householder, 'The Teacher says, Where is my guest room, where I am to eat the passover with my disciples?' [15]And he will show you a large upper room furnished and ready; there prepare for us." [16]And the disciples set out and went to the city, and found it as he had told them; and they prepared the passover.

[17]And when it was evening he came with the twelve. [18]And as they were at table eating, Jesus said, "Truly, I say to you, one of you will betray me, one who is eating with me." [19]They began to be sorrowful, and to say to him one after another, "Is it I?" [20]He said to them, "It is one of the twelve, one who is dipping bread into the dish with me. [21]For the Son of man goes as it is written of him, but woe to that man by whom the Son of man is betrayed! It would have been better for that man if he had not been born."

[22]And as they were eating, he took bread, and blessed, and broke it, and gave it to them, and said, "Take; this is my body." [23]And he took a cup, and when he had given thanks he gave it to them, and they all drank of it. [24]And he said to them, "This is my blood of the covenant, which is poured out for many. [25]Truly, I say to you, I shall not drink again of the fruit of the vine until that day when I drink it new in the kingdom of God."

[26]And when they had sung a hymn, they went out to the Mount of Olives. [27]And Jesus said to them, "You will all fall away; for it is written, 'I will strike the shepherd, and the sheep will be scattered." [28]But after I am raised up, I will go before you to Galilee." [29]Peter said to him, "Even though they all fall away, I will not." [30]And Jesus said to him, "Truly, I say to you, this very night, before the cock crows twice, you will deny me three times." [31]But he said vehemently, "If I must die with you, I will not deny you." And they all said the same. (14:12-31)

A) PREPARATION FOR THE PASSOVER (14:12-17)

A day has passed and it is now Thursday, the day before the Passover. In the afternoon the lambs for the Passover feast were slaughtered at the temple. In the evening the festival began and the Passover meals would be celebrated in Jerusalem. The story is aware of all this: the day is noted as "the first day of Unleavened Bread, when they sacrificed the Passover lamb" (14:12). As we already suggested, Mark refers to Thursday the fourteenth of Nisan, even though strictly speaking the first day of Unleavened Bread began in the evening, the start of the fifteenth day of Nisan.[11]

The account of the preparation will repeatedly refer to the Passover (14:12 [2X], 14, 16) clearly indicating that Mark understands the meal that follows as a Passover meal (even though the description of the meal itself does not necessarily identify it as a Passover celebration). The symbol of Passover does not seem to be exploited by Mark in the remainder of his passion account (in contrast to John) but in these preparatory scenes, he brings that rich theological symbol of liberation and hope emphatically before the reader.

The detailed and somewhat unusual instructions given to the disciples by Jesus and their literal fulfillment (14:16) are reminiscent of a previous entry into Jerusalem. In 11:1-7, two disciples were instructed to go into a nearby village to procure the colt for Jesus' triumphant entry into the Holy City. Now two are sent again (14:13), presumably from Bethany where Jesus and the disciples remain (14:3). This time they are sent into Jerusalem itself. They are told they will be met by a man carrying a water jar (an unusual sight since this was usually the work of women). They are to follow him to the place where the Passover will be held. The master of the household (and presumably the master of the servant carrying the water jar) would show them the room where the feast was to be prepared. The two disciples carry out their instructions and find all as Jesus had foretold (14:16).

The whole mood of this piece demonstrates Jesus' deliberateness and assurance in the face of impending death. This, in fact, is the mood of the entire supper sequence in which Jesus' ultimate triumph over betrayal, desertion and

---

[11] Cf. above, pp. 43-44.

death itself is vigorously proclaimed. Beginning with Gethsemane, however, a more somber and distressful mood will
be struck in the passion account.

At evening Jesus enters the city with the twelve to celebrate Passover (14:12). This quiet, almost guarded entry, is
in contrast to the triumphant procession that brought Jesus
the first time from Bethany to Jerusalem in Mark's account
(11:1-10). Now the threat of the plot against Jesus gives this
moment an eerie stillness, as if before the storm.

B) PREDICTION OF BETRAYAL (14:18-21)

The Passover meal begins on a somber note. Just as the
woman's beautiful act of discipleship was starkly framed by
acts of treachery, so the final meal is surrounded by Jesus'
prophetic predictions of betrayal, desertion, and denial.
What the reader had already been informed of (cf. 3:19 and
especially 14:10-11) is now revealed to have been known by
Jesus. His prophetic knowledge is contrasted with the
baffled shock of the disciples (14:19).

The whole thrust of the scene is to interpret Judas' act as a
betrayal of friendship. The poignant phrases heap up: "one
of you," "one who is eating with me," "one of the twelve,"
"one who is dipping bread into the dish with me." Conversely, Jesus himself is portrayed as one betrayed and deserted
by his friends. Verses 18 and 20 paraphrase Psalm 41:9 —
"Even my bosom friend in whom I trust, who ate of my
bread, has lifted his heel against me." (There is a similar
echo in Psalm 55:12-14). This motif of betrayal by friends
was part of a Jewish tradition reflecting on the sufferings of
the Just One, who is abandoned and tormented, his only
hope being God's fidelity. This Old Testament motif has
influenced the Synoptic passion traditions, especially those
of Matthew and Luke.[12]

---

[12] For a thorough discussion of this tradition, cf. L. Ruppert, *Jesus als der leidende
Gerechte? Der Weg Jesu im Lichte eines alt-und zwischen-testamentlichen Motivs*
(Stuttgarter Bibelstudien 59; Stuttgart: KBW, 1972). R. Pesch, *Das Markusevan-
gelium*, repeatedly appeals to this motif as a basic ingredient of Mark's passion
narrative. While the motif is present, Pesch may overemphasize its importance for
Mark's theology.

The frightened question of the other apostles — "Is it I?" (14:19) — reveals the point of this incident. The prediction displays Jesus' prophetic knowledge of the impending events and casts around him the mantle of the suffering Just One. But it also puts a glaring spotlight on mortal failure within the circle of the Twelve. The Christian reader cannot avoid repeating (note: "one after another") the anguished question of the apostles: "Is it I?" The power of the passion drama lies precisely in such invitations for the reader to participate.

The scene concludes with what is in effect another in the series of Son of Man sayings that have lined Mark's story since the encounter at Caesarea Philippi (8:31).[13] This one is tersely stated: "The Son of Man goes as it is written of him" (14:21). No details are needed since the event of betrayal, arrest, torture and death (the content of the passion predictions in 8:31; 9:31 and 10:33-34) are now unfolding.

Even though the Son of Man goes his God-appointed way of humiliation and exaltation, the responsibility of the betrayer is not diminished. One senses here the inevitable tension between the bedrock biblical conviction of God's sovereignty over all events, not least that of Jesus' death, and the Bible's equally tenacious claim on human freedom and responsibility. Judas' destined role in the drama of salvation does not reduce him to a helpless marionette; he chooses betrayal and must be responsible.

C) THE MEAL (14:22-25)

This scene is one of the most vibrant theological crescendos in Mark's Gospel. Here Jesus will interpret the ultimate significance of his death. An avalanche of literature has flowed from scholarly examination of this and the other New Testament institution texts (cf. Mt 26:26-29; Lk 22:14-20; Jn 6:51; I Cor 11:23-26).[14] It should be noted, however,

---

[13] Cf. above, pp. 28-35.

[14] See, for example, J. Jeremias, *The Eucharistic Words of Jesus* (New York: Scribner, 1966); R. Pesch, *Das Abendmahl und Jesu Todesverstandnis* (Quaestiones Disputatae 80; Friburg: Herder, 1978); X. Léon-Dufour, *Le partage du pain eucharistique: Selon le Nouveau Testament* (Parole de Dieu; Paris: Editions du Cerf, 1982).

that Mark, in contrast to Paul (see I Cor 11:23-26), does not present the supper tradition explicitly as a grounding for the community's celebration of Eucharist. Undoubtedly the scene would evoke reflection on the ultimate origin and meaning of the eucharistic cult for any Christian reader, but Mark's immediate purpose in the context of the passion narrative is to use this scene as an interpretation of Jesus' entire mission and of the disciples' stake in it. It is on this level of meaning we will dwell.

The flow of the narrative is clear. In the course of the meal, Jesus performs a symbolic gesture of blessing and sharing bread and wine with his disciples.[15] The meaning of the scene is carried by the interpretive words that Jesus pronounces after each action and at the conclusion of the scene. We will examine each in turn.

The Bread

The bread, blessed and broken, is followed by the words: "This is my body" (v.22). In so doing the Marcan Jesus uses the bread as a profound symbol of his own person and mission. In tracing the term "bread" or "loaves" in the Gospel we find that Mark has already used it as a potent symbol of Jesus' messianic mission.

In 6:34-44 Mark narrates the first of two feeding stories. Accompanied by his disciples who have just returned from their mission (6:30-32), Jesus comes ashore to find a throng waiting for him. Mark significantly notes Jesus' compassion for them: "he had compassion on them, because they were like sheep without a shepherd." In response to their need

---

[15] The entire scene is tersely narrated. Accompanying each element is an interpretive word (14:22,24). Over each element a prayer of blessing is said by Jesus but the contents of the blessing are unexpressed: *eulogēsas* ("blessing") the bread (v.22), *eucharistēsas* ("giving thanks") with the wine (v.23). The two actions have an interlocking structure. In the action over the bread the disciples are tersely commanded: "Take (it)." This is assumed but not stated with the cup. Conversely, after the offering of the cup it is reported that "they all drank of it" (v.23); this is assumed but not stated about the bread. Note that in each case the disciples' direct participation in the action (the command to share in the bread and the cup and the actual carrying out of the command) is clearly stressed. The scene closes with a solemn "amen" word.

Jesus began to teach them (6:34) and ultimately to feed them, over the protests of his uncomprehending disciples. The five loaves and two fish are blessed and distributed to a crowd of more than 5,000. Although the story mentions bread and fish, it is the loaves that become the focus (cf. 6:37, 41, 44). Even more significantly the actions of Jesus are directly related to the actions over the loaves at the Passover meal:

6:41	and taking (*kai labōn*)	. . the loaves (*tous artous*)
14:22	and taking (*labōn*)	bread (*arton*)
6:41	he blessed (*eulogēsan*)	. . broke (*kateklasen*)
		. . gave (*edidou*)
14:22	having blessed (*eulogēsas*)	. . he broke (*eklasen*)
		. . gave (*edōken*)

The disciples figure prominently. They receive the blessed loaves (and fish) from Jesus to give it to the crowds, and they are the ones who gather the leftover fragments into twelve baskets (6:43).

The miraculous feeding is an obvious display of Jesus' messianic work. The hapless and disoriented throngs are fed with an abundance of food through the compassion of Jesus. The leftovers fill *twelve* baskets, reminiscent of the twelve tribes of Israel to be gathered on the day of salvation. Jesus' mighty work recalls that of the great prophet Elijah who miraculously fed the widow and her son on meagre rations of barley and oil (I Kings 17:8-16; see a similar event in the life of Elisha, II Kings 4:1-7, 42-44). It evokes, too, the exodus refrain: the hungry people are in a *desert* (Mk 6:35) and are fed just as God fed Israel with the abundant manna (see especially Exodus 16:32 — And Moses said, "This is what the Lord has commanded: 'Let an omer of it be kept throughout your generations, that they may see the bread with which I fed you in the wilderness, when I brought you out of the land of Egypt.' ").

The second feeding story occurs in Mark 8:1-10. The same elements are present. Jesus is touched with compas-

sion for the hunger of the crowds (8:2-3), while his disciples
miss the mark (8:4). The setting is the desert (8:4). In this
instance the loaves completely dominate the scenario (the
fish are mentioned only incidentally in v. 7). The crowd now
numbers four thousand and there are seven baskets of fragments left over (8:8).

Once again the explicit connection to the Passover meal is
made:

   8:6   taking (*lābon*) ... bread (*artous*)
 14:22 taking (*lābon*) ... bread (*arton*)
   8:6   giving thanks (*eucharistēsos*) he broke (*eklasen*) and
            gave (*kai edōken*)
 14:22 (cf. 14:23, "having given thanks") he broke (*eklasen*)
            and gave (*kai edōken*)

As in chapter 6 the disciples' role is significant: the disciples are given the blessed loaves to distribute to the crowd
(8:6) and they collect the leftover fragments (8:8).

The duplication of the stories is not pointless but is used
by Mark to give another level of meaning to the feedings.
The story in chapter 6 takes place in *Jewish* territory.[16]
Beginning in 7:24, however, in seeming reaction to his conflict with the Pharisees and Scribes (7:1-2), Jesus begins a
journey through *Gentile* territory from Tyre and Sidon and
into the Decapolis (7:24,31). The feeding story in 8:1-10 caps
that Gentile mission; in 8:11 he will return to Dalmanutha
on the western (that is, Jewish) shore and once again
encounter Jewish opponents (8:11-13).

The feedings, therefore, take place on two sides of the
lake, one Jewish and the other Gentile, in Mark's configura-

---

[16] In 6:1 Jesus is in his home region of Nazareth; afterwards he continues his
mission in the surrounding territory (6:6). Following the sea story of 6:45-52, Jesus
and his disciples land at Gennesaret (6:53) on the western (Jewish) side of the Lake.
The dispute with the Pharisees (7:1-23) and Jesus' subsequent departure for the
Gentile regions of Tyre and Sidon (7:24) indicate that all of the material in chapter
6, including the feeding, has been in a *Jewish* context. On this section of Mark's
Gospel and its connection with the institution account, cf. D. Senior, "The
Eucharist in Mark: Mission, Reconciliation, Hope," *Biblical Theology Bulletin* 12
(1982), 67-72, and N. Beck, "Reclaiming a Biblical Text: The Mark 8:14-21
Discussion about Bread in the Boat," *Catholic Biblical Quarterly* 43 (1981), 57-75.

tion. Jesus feeds both Jew and Gentile, indicating the universal scope of his mission. The numbers of the baskets seem to reflect this differentiation: at the end of the Jewish feeding *twelve* baskets are gathered, symbolizing the assembled gathering of Israel (6:43). At the conclusion of the Gentile feeding, *seven* are gathered (8:8) a number that can mean universality or completion.

This meaning of the loaves as a symbol of Jesus' universal mission is clearly important to Mark. This is indicated by the fact that it is the *loaves* that are misunderstood by the disciples. The failure of the disciples to recognize Jesus in the sea story of 6:45-52 is explained, "for they did not understand about the *loaves*, but their hearts were hardened" (6:52). Mark seems to make the disciples' misunderstanding of the meaning of the loaves equivalent to failure to understand Jesus himself! The same point is made but with greater force in 8:14-21, the conclusion to the entire Galilean ministry of Jesus. Once again in the context of a sea story, the disciples misunderstand Jesus' reference to the "leaven of the Pharisees and the leaven of Herod" (8:15). They erroneously believe he is chiding them for having brought only one loaf of bread with them in the boat (8:14,16). They exclaim to each other: "we have no loaves" (8:16). The story's focus on bread seems, in fact, quite awkward and contrived except for the fact that Mark intends to stress its symbolic meaning. Jesus' vigorously indicts the disciples for their failure to understand:

[17]And being aware of it, Jesus said to them, "Why do you discuss the fact that you have no bread? Do you not yet perceive or understand? Are your hearts hardened? [18]Having eyes do you not see, and having ears do you not hear? And do you not remember? [19]When I broke the five loaves for the five thousand, how many baskets full of broken pieces did you take up?" They said to him, "[20]Twelve." And the seven for the four thousand, how many baskets full of broken pieces did you take up?" And they said to him, "Seven." [21]And he said to them, "Do you not yet understand?" (Mk 8:17-21)

The meaning of the feeding stories as action summaries of
Jesus' entire mission to Israel and to the nations is clearly in
mind here. To fail to grasp their meaning is to fail to
comprehend Jesus himself; thus Mark uses blindness and
deafness as metaphors of failed faith just as had already
been done in the parable discourse of chapter 4.[17]
Thus "loaves" or "bread" (the same Greek word, *artos* is
used throughout in Mark) is clearly established in Mark's
Gospel as a symbol of Jesus' mission to gather and nourish
the scattered people of Israel and to break beyond these
boundaries to feed the Gentiles as well. The Syro-Phoenician
woman had pleaded for a portion of that "bread," and
through her tenacious faith received it for her daughter (Mk 7:24-
30). But in 8:14-21 the disciples fail to understand that the one
"bread" Jesus provides is sufficient to feed all of the multitudes,
Jewish and Gentile. The setting of a meal in the *desert* and
the evident abundance of the feast widens the symbolism.
God's feeding of Israel during the Exodus is evoked as well
as the longed-for messianic banquet on Zion. This messianic
symbolism had already been in play when Jesus had called
Levi and dined with him and other outcasts (2:15-17).[18]

The supper in 14:22-25 is, therefore, the *third* in a series of
messianic meals in the Gospel. The ritualized action of Jesus
over the loaves — blessing, breaking, distributing — is the
same in each. In each, the disciples play major roles. Each,
too, has some connection with the liberating exodus: the
first two by their desert setting, the last by its connection
with Passover. But the last meal brings an even greater
depth to the loaves' significance. Not only are the loaves
signs of Jesus' inclusive mission; now the loaf *is his body*, his
very self (14:22).[19] Jesus faces onrushing death; his "body" is

---

[17] "To you has been given the secret of the kingdom of God, but for those outside
everything is in parables; so that they may indeed see but not perceive, and may
indeed hear but not understand; lest they should turn again, and be forgiven" (Mk
4:11-12). This verse is a paraphrase of Isaiah 6:9-10.

[18] Cf. above, p. 55.

[19] R. Pesch notes that such an interpretive word fits the style of the Passover meal
and the Exodus story itself where Moses declares over the manna, "It is the bread
which the Lord has given you to eat" (Ex 16:15). See R. Pesch, *Der Markusevangelium*, II, 355.

about to be handed over, tortured, broken, put to death. At this point the offering of bread-declared-body to the disciples becomes a vivid symbol of Jesus' death for others. The bread word joins with the passion predictions that lined the Gospel declaring that the Son of Man would be "handed over." Above all the offering of body/bread harmonizes with that fundamental statement of 10:45 — "The Son of Man came not to be served but to serve, and to give his life as a ransom for many." The breaking of the loaves for the crowds expressed the ultimate meaning of Jesus' messianic work; the word at the meal affirms that Jesus' death is the final act of that mission, self-donation "for the many."

The Cup

The "cup," too, has symbolic meaning in the Gospel, although not as extensively as that of the bread. In this instance, however, the interpretive word of 14:24 is much more explicit.

The "cup" was used in 10:38-39 to refer to Jesus' death. "To drink the cup God had mixed" was a Jewish expression for the martyrdom a prophet had to endure and, from the context of 10:35-45, it is clear that Mark, too, intends the reference to the cup in this way.[20] The crass ambition of Zebedee's sons drives them to seek places of power at Jesus' side. But Jesus checks them with a reminder of what sharing in his power entails: "Are you able to drink the cup that I drink, or to be baptized with the baptism with which I am baptized?" (10:45). The "cup" as symbolic of the death of Jesus is confirmed by the prayer in Gethsemane. Jesus prays that the Father would "remove the cup" (14:36).

The link between 10:35-45 and 14:22-25 is striking not only because of the cup symbolism but because in both instances the disciples are invited to share in Jesus' sacrifi-

---

[20] The quotation is from the Ascension of Isaiah (5:13), a Christian version of an earlier Jewish work, the Martyrdom of Isaiah. On the symbolic use of "cup" in Judaism and early Christianity, cf. L. Goppelt in G. Kittel (ed.), *Theological Dictionary of the New Testament* Vol. VI (Grand Rapids: Wm. B. Eerdmans, 1968), 148-58.

cial death for the world. In the supper scene, following upon Jesus' presumed command the disciples "all drink of it" (the cup). The interpretive words spell out what the action of Jesus had already communicated: "This is my blood of the covenant, which is poured out for many" (14:24). His approaching death, his blood poured out, is a "death for many." The term "for many" is, in semitic idiom, a universally inclusive term, and, as with a similar phrase in 10:45, seems to portray Jesus' death as the atoning death of the Servant of Yahweh.[21]

The phrase "of the covenant" draws another related line of biblical metaphors into the rich theological tapestry of the institution account. The phrase evokes Exodus 24:8 when Moses ratified the covenant by taking the blood of sacrificial oxen, sprinkling half of it on the altar and the other half on the people: "Behold the blood of the covenant which the Lord has made with you in accordance with all these words." Some manuscript traditions read "the *new* covenant" in Mark 14:24, but this is probably a later assimilation to the Pauline (I Cor 11:25) and Lucan (22:20) versions. But even without the word present the idea of the new, eschatological covenant proclaimed by Jeremiah harmonizes with Mark's entire thought here:

> [31]Behold, the days are coming, says the Lord, when I will make a new covenant with the house of Israel and the house of Judah, [32]not like the covenant which I made with their fathers when I took them by the hand to bring them out of the land of Egypt, my covenant which they broke, though I was their husband, says the Lord. [33]But this is the covenant which I will make with the house of Israel after those days, says the Lord: I will put my law within them, and I will write it upon their hearts; and I will be their God, and they will be my people. [39]And no longer shall each man teach his neighbor and each his brother, saying, "Know the Lord,' for they shall all know

---

[21] The Servant is blessed "because he poured out his soul to death and was numbered with the transgressors; yet he bore the sins *of many* and made intercession for the transgressors" (Isaiah 53:12).

me, from the least of them to the greatest, says the Lord;
for I will forgive their iniquity, and I will remember their
sin no more." (Jeremiah 31:31-34)

Jesus' redemptive death effects the new and definitive
covenant renewal awaited by Israel. It would be a time of
forgiveness, an experience that the Son of Man had already
brought through his mission of compassion for those
broken by sin (see, especially, Mk 2:1-12, 15-17).

Death and Victory

The supper scene is punctuated with a solemn "amen"
saying (v.25) that recapitulates the meal symbolism of the
words over the bread and wine and casts them into a final
passion and resurrection prediction.

Jesus states that this meal is his last: "I shall not drink
again of the fruit of the vine."[22] The poignancy and finality
of this Passover eve strike home. No longer shall Jesus
celebrate this meal of hope and joy with his disciples.

But coupled to the prediction of separation and death is a
defiant "until" that bridges the chasm of death and projects
Jesus into the banquet of the Kingdom. In spite of death he
will share in the banquet on Zion for which Israel longed,
the banquet where the wine of the Kingdom would flow
anew and God would brush aside the cobweb of death and
wipe away all tears.[23] The verse is a stunning prediction of
hope and victory planted in a story that rushes toward
death.[24]

The evangelist has used the supper scene to confront the
reader with a powerful theological interpretation of the
death of Jesus. Jesus' death is the definitive act of his entire
mission: it is a giving of life that bears away the burden of sin

---

[22] The "fruit of the vine" is used in the Bible as a poetic expression for wine: see, for
example, Numbers 6:4; Isaiah 32:12; Habakkuk 3:7, etc.

[23] See, for example, Isaiah 25:6-8; 65:17-25; I Enoch 62:14, etc.

[24] Some commentators note that the language of this verse is notably different in
style from the Son of Man passion predictions in which contact with the details of
the passion story itself is clearly evident. This verse with its symbols of wine and the
banquet of the Kingdom smacks of the historical Jesus.

from the world and renews the covenant between God and humanity. It is the final work of God's Christ drawing together the hopeless and scattered people of God — Israel and the nations — and feeding them with bread. It is an act of hope that proclaims that the cup of death will be transformed into wine drunk triumphantly in the Kingdom of God. All of these characteristic themes of Mark have, as well, kinship with the spirit of the Passover festival, with its memory of liberation from Egypt and the covenant in the desert, with its binding of Israel as one people and its enduring hope for the coming of God's rule.

D) PREDICTIONS OF DISCIPLESHIP BROKEN AND RENEWED (14:26-31)

The Passover scenes conclude with predictions of desertion (v.27) and denial (v.30) that veer sharply from the stress on the bond between master and disciple so solemnly celebrated in the previous scene. Mark continues to show his knack for lacing a scene with jolting counterpoints. But the scene also continues the strong if muted sense of ultimate victory that characterizes the Passover incidents. After his resurrection Jesus will lead his disciples to Galilee (v.28). By means of all these predictions Mark demonstrates Jesus' prophetic knowledge of the events about to transpire.

The scene opens with the singing of a hymn, no doubt the "Hallel," selections from Psalms 114 to 118 that traditionally ended the Passover meal. Jesus and his disciples are on the way to Gethsemane (v.32) on the western slopes of the Mount of Olives. Custom demanded that the Passover festival be celebrated within the environs of Jerusalem; the Kedron valley and the western slope of the Mount of Olives facing the Holy City fulfilled that requirement. The march to Gethsemane and the singing of the Hallel, therefore, mark the conclusion of the Passover scenes and provide transition to the awesome events that are about to take place in the olive grove.

The prediction of the disciples' desertion comes with stunning bluntness: "You will all be scandalized (in me)," the literal sense of the word *scandalisthēsesthe*, which the RSV interprets as "fall away." The sense of the Greek word means "to be an *obstacle*," or "to cause offense." Mark has already used this verb in his Gospel to mean encountering a difficulty or obstacle that blocks one's faith. Despite Jesus' power to heal, the people of his own city, Nazareth, refuse to believe in him. Their own familiarity with Jesus causes them to take offense at him. ("Is this not the carpenter, the son of Mary and brother of James and Joses and Judas and Simon, and are not his sisters here with us?" Mk 6:3). They were, Mark observes, "scandalized in him" (6:3). An even more pertinent text is found in the parable discourse where Jesus explains the parable of the sower (4:14-20). The fate of the seed falling on rocky ground is like those who, at first, accept the gospel with joy but their discipleship has no roots and they persevere only for a while. When "tribulation or persecution arises on account of the word" these rootless disciples "immediately are scandalized" (4:16-17).

There is little doubt that Mark has this text in mind as he narrates the prediction of 14:27. As we have noted, the passion story is not simply about the passion of Jesus, but the passion the community experiences in its living out of the gospel in the world.[25] Now the disciples who have "heard the word with joy"(4:16), yet whose faith in Jesus is not deep enough to be ready for the encounter with suffering and death, will collapse under the crisis: "they will all be scandalized." In Mark's sober account (in contrast to Luke and John) none of the chosen disciples will remain with Jesus until the moment of his death.[26] The disciples will bolt from the garden in panic (14:50-51) and Peter will swear that he is not Jesus' disciple (14:66-72).

A citation from Zechariah 13:7 seals the prediction and indicates that even this grim moment of failure is myste-

[25] Cf. above, pp. 37-39.

[26] Luke seems to downplay the disciples' desertion of Jesus at the arrest by omitting any mention of their flight. Luke also places the "multitudes" and some of Jesus' "acquaintances" with the faithful women at the cross (cf. Lk 23:48-49). In John's account the Beloved Disciple is present at the cross, along with the mother of Jesus and other women (see Jn 19:25-27). At the arrest John has the disciples sent away by Jesus rather than flee (Jn 18:8-9).

riously part of the divine plan: "I will strike the shepherd and the sheep will be scattered"(14:27). The original context of the Old Testament citation is a series of oracles (cf. Zechariah 12-13) warning of God's chastisement of Jerusalem and calling the people to repentance.[27] Mark (or possibly Christian tradition before him) freely adapts the words of Zechariah to fit the context of the passion story. The original quotation has Yahweh himself say, "Strike the Shepherd, that the sheep may be scattered" (Zechariah 13:7). Mark's version ("*I* will strike the Shepherd") continues the emphasis of the original on the divine initiative. In the mystery of God's sovereignty the death of Jesus is no tragic accident or triumph of evil. The life that would flow from the death and resurrection of Jesus guaranteed that even the dark moment of crucifixion was somehow according to God' unfathomable plan of salvation. But another dimension of the original quotation is pointedly changed. From Mark's perspective, the striking of the Shepherd was *not* for the purpose of scattering the sheep (as in the original quote from Zechariah: "Strike the shepherd *so that* the sheep may be scattered", quite different from Mark's "and the sheep will be scattered.") The disciples' failure is a consequence but not the purpose of Jesus' death.

"Sheep" and "shepherd" were long-standing biblical metaphors for Israel and its leaders. God himself was a "shepherd" who cared for and led Israel to refreshment (see, for example, Psalm 23; Ezekiel 34). So, too, were the great leaders of Israel to be responsible "shepherds" for the people. Moses implored God to appoint Joshua as leader so that the assembly of Israel "may not be as sheep which have no shepherd" (Num 27:17). The Davidic Messiah who would come to liberate Israel on the final day was also spoken of as a true shepherd whom God would set in charge

[27] The same passage seems to be alluded to in John 16:32. The oracles of Zechariah are also cited in John 19:37 ("They shall look on him whom they have expeierced"- cf. Zechariah 12:10), suggesting that this Old Testament book was a traditional part of early Christian reflection on the passion of Jesus. On this, cf. F. F. Bruce, "The Book of Zechariah and the Passion Narrative," *Bulletin of the John Rylands University Library of Manchester* 43 (1960), 342-45.

of his sheep (Ezekiel 34:23-24; also Jeremiah 23:4), unlike the false shepherds who abused the sheep (Ezekiel 34:1-16). Mark had already applied this metaphor to Jesus in the Gospel by noting his compassion for the crowds prior to the first story of the multiplication of the loaves: "he had compassion on them, because they were like sheep without a shepherd" (Mark 6:34).

Now in the paradox of the cross the shepherd would lay down his life for the sheep, and the disciples, not yet responsive to the way of God, would scatter in disillusionment and fear.

Seldom in Mark are Jesus' predictions of death or failure left unrelieved; here, too, the prediction of Jesus' death and the disciples' failure is immediately followed by a prediction of resurrection and discipleship renewal (14:28). "But after I am raised up, I will go before you to Galilee." It is a key verse in Mark's Gospel with important implications for interpreting the final thrust of the entire story. This promise of Jesus will be repeated by the heavenly messenger who greets the women at the tomb (16:7): they are to proclaim to the disciples and Peter "that he is going before you to Galilee; there you will see him."[28]

The return to Galilee catches up a major motif of Mark. Galilee was the place of mission, the arena where Jesus' exorcisms and healings had broken the bonds of evil. There, too, the disciples had been called and commissioned to take up Jesus' proclamation of the coming rule of God.[29] But Jesus had not remained in Galilee. The way of the Son of

---

[28] Cf. below, pp. 135-137. The importance of the promise of Jesus in 14:27 may be underestimated in some current interpretations of the Gospel. Some authors consider the silence and fear of the women as they leave the tomb as a final instance of discipleship failure (16:8). The disciples therefore do not get the Easter message and remain alienated from Jesus (see, for example, N. Perrin, *The Resurrection According to Matthew, Mark, and Luke* [Philadelphia: Fortress, 1977], 14-38). This line of interpretation allows an ambivalent text (the meaning of the women's silence in 16:8) to cancel out the *unambivalent* promise of reconciliation spoken by the Marcan Jesus and repeated by the messenger at the tomb (14:28; 16:7). On this point, see the comments of E. Best, *Following Jesus*, 199-203.

[29] Cf. above, pp. 28-35.

Man was to go up to Jerusalem, to validate his mission and to give it ultimate expression in the laying down of his life. In the final and most detailed of the passion predictions which punctuate that fateful journey, Mark described the configuration of Christian discipleship:

> ³²"And they were on the road, going up to Jerusalem, and Jesus was *going ahead of them*; and they were amazed, and those who followed were afraid. And taking the twelve again, he began to tell them what was to happen to him, ³³saying, "Behold, we are going up to Jerusalem; and the Son of man will be delivered to the chief priests and the scribes, and they will condemn him to death, and deliver him to the Gentiles; ³⁴and they will mock him, and spit upon him, and scourge him, and kill him; and after three days he will rise." (10:32-34)

The word *proagōn* "to go ahead of" or "lead" used in 10:32 is identical with the words found in 14:28 ("I will go before" or "lead") and 16:7 ("he is leading"). The three verses together are a distillation of Mark's entire theology: the Son of Man who leads the fearful community of disciples from Galilee to Jerusalem and who will also go ahead of them through death to victory, is the same compassionate and now triumphant Son of Man who will restore his broken followers to discipleship and lead them back to Galilee. "Galilee" is the place of the universal mission, but no disciples are ready to proclaim the Gospel there until they have walked the road to Jerusalem and encountered the reality of the cross.

Mark's whiplash technique of juxtaposing words of hope with vignettes of failure continues as the prediction of Peter's denial now moves into focus. Peter, the first called (1:16-18) protests that even if the others fail he will not. His words directly contradict Jesus' prediction:

v.27 *"you will all* be scandalized"

v.29 "even if all will be scandalized, *I will not*"

Jesus reaffirms his prediction of Peter's failure, but now

with a solemn "amen" saying that sketches the precise details of the leading disciple's "scandal" (14:30) which will take place during the Jewish trial (see below, 14:66-72). The reference to the cockcrow recalls the warning of 13:35-36, "watch...lest he come and find you asleep." Peter's bravado matches his blindness. The reader knows that this was the disciple who called Jesus the "Christ," but attempted to silence that "Christ" when Jesus began to speak of the Son of Man having to face death (Mark 8:31-33). The inability to "take up the cross" (8:34) would be the deadly scandal for Peter and he would deny his master in ironically true words: "I *do not know* this man of whom you speak" (14:71).

Peter's vehement rebuttal of Jesus' prediction (14:31) — "If I must die with you, I will not deny you" — and the joining of all the other disciples in this protest form an ironic conclusion to the scene. As on the road to Jerusalem, the disciples once again prove deaf to Jesus' words about the cross. Instead of a plea for mercy or strength (in the spirit of the blind Bartimaeus who sought sight and received it, 10:46-52), the disciples merely demonstrate their obtuseness. The reader knows that the prophetic words of Jesus will prove true and the crisis of the arrest will wash out the shallow loyalty of the disciples. The same tragic fulfillment would follow upon Jesus' prediction of Judas' betrayal at the start of the meal. But the reader also knows that while prophecies of weakness and failure would prove true, so, too, would Jesus' prophetic words about triumph over death and ultimate reconciliation with his disciples in Galilee.

III. Gethsemane: Prayer and Arrest (14:32-52)

The change to a new setting, from the Passover meal in the upper room to Gethsemane on the western slope of the Mount of Olives, signals another segment of Mark's passion story. Motifs of christology and discipleship continue to dominate the narrative. Jesus' vigilant prayer stands in contrast to the sleep of the disciples (14:32-42); when Jesus faces his captors at the moment of betrayal, the disciples scurry away in panic (14:43-52). The crisis of the passion has begun.

[32]And they went to a place which was called Gethsemane; and he said to his disciples, "Sit here, while I pray."[33]And he took with him Peter and James and John, and began to be greatly distressed and troubled. [34]And he said to them, "My soul is very sorrowful, even to death; remain here, and watch." [35]And going a little farther, he fell on the ground and prayed that, if it were possible, the hour might pass from him. [36]And he said, "Abba, Father, all things are possible to thee; remove this cup from me; yet not what I will, but what thou wilt." [37]And he came and found them sleeping, and he said to Peter, "Simon, are you asleep? Could you not watch one hour? [38]Watch and pray that you may not enter into temptation; the spirit indeed is willing, but the flesh is weak." [39]And again he went away and prayed, saying the same words. [40]And again he came and found them sleeping, for their eyes were very heavy; and they did not know what to answer him. [41]And he came the third time, and said to them, "Are you still sleeping and taking your rest? It is enough; the hour has come; the Son of man is betrayed into the hands of sinners. [42]Rise, let us be going; see, my betrayer is at hand."

[43]And immediately, while he was still speaking, Judas came, one of the twelve, and with him a crowd with swords and clubs, from the chief priests and the scribes and the elders. [44]Now the betrayer had given them a sign, saying, "The one I shall kiss is the man; seize him and lead him away under guard." [45]And when he came, he went up to him at once, and said, "Master!" And he kissed him. [46]And they laid hands on him and seized him. [47]But one of those who stood by drew his sword, and struck the slave of the high priest and cut off his ear. [48]And Jesus said to them, "Have you come out as against a robber, with swords and clubs to capture me? [49]Day after day I was

with you in the temple teaching, and you did not seize me. But let the scriptures be fulfilled." [50]And they all forsook him and fled. [51]And a young man followed him, with nothing but a linen cloth about his body; and they seized him, [52]but he left the linen cloth and ran away naked. (14:32-52)

A) PRAYER IN GETHSEMANE (14:32-42)

This is one of the Gospel's most exquisite and haunting scenes. Before the specter of death Jesus prays with deep anguish while around him his trusted disciples sleep, unaware of the momentous events that are about to explode. Studies abound on the possible historical origins of this scene and the possibility that Mark has combined two or more pre-existing accounts to give it its present form.[30] Our focus will be on the meaning of the Gethsemane scene from Mark's perspective. From this vantage point, the text betrays few jagged edges and, indeed, fits smoothly into the ongoing narrative of Mark.

Preparation for prayer begins with the arrival at Gethsemane, a name which means "olive press" (John 18:1 speaks of a "garden" and we may presume that Mark, too, envisages a garden or secluded grove of olive trees on the slope of the mountain). The disciples are instructed to sit and wait for him while he goes to pray.[31] The significance of

[30] See, for example, R. Barbour, "Gethsemane in the Tradition of the Passion," *New Testament Studies* 16 (1969/70) 231-51; J. W. Holleron, *The Synoptic Gethsemane: A Critical Study* (Analecta Gregoriana; Rome: Gregorian University, 1973); D. Stanley, *Jesus in Gethsemane* (New York: Paulist, 1980). For a study of Mark's redactional work in the Gethsemane scene, cf. W. H. Kelber, "Mark 14, 32-42: Gethsemane Passion Christology and Discipleship Failure," *Zeitschrift für neuentestamentliche Wissenschaft* 63 (1972), 166-87 and his later work, "The Hour of the Son of Man and The Temptation of the Disciples," in *The Passion in Mark* (W. Kelber ed.; Philadelphia: Fortress, 1976), 41-60.

[31] Some commentators see here an allusion to Genesis 22:5 where Abraham in preparation for the sacrifice of Isaac instructs his servants, "Stay here with the ass; I and the lad will go yonder and worship, and come again to you." Although some allusion to the sacrifice of Isaac cannot be rule out, the wording used at this point in the Gospel of Matthew (see Mt. 26:36) suggests that it was more to the fore for this evangelist than for Mark.

the moment is signaled by Jesus' taking with him Peter, James and John (14:33). This same trio had been the privileged witnesses of the raising of Jairus' daughter from the dead (5:37) and the transfiguration (9:2). And these three, along with Andrew (13:3), had heard Jesus' final discourse on the Mount of Olives, predicting the travails of the community in history and ending with a warning "to stay awake!" (13:37). Now these disciples who had witnessed the high points of his ministry would be with the Son of Man as he begins his passion.

The Prayer of Jesus

The focus of the scene falls first on Jesus and his prayer (14:33b-36). With stunning boldness Mark presents Jesus as engulfed in the prayer of lament. In the tradition of the just ones of Israel — anguished before death, tormented by the betrayal of friends, vulnerable to enemies — Jesus clings to the one thread that gives ultimate meaning to his existence, his faith in the God of Israel.[32] The scene pulls at the taproot of biblical faith. Such laments shudder through the psalms, many of which have verbal echoes in the Gethsemane scene:

> 8 To thee, O Lord, I cried;
>   and to the Lord I made supplication
> 9 "What profit is there in my death,
>   if I go down to the Pit?
>   Will the dust praise thee?
>   Will it tell of thy faithfulness?
> 10 Hear, O Lord, and be gracious to me!
>   O Lord, be thou my helper!" (Ps 30:8-10)

> 11 Do not thou, O Lord, withhold
>   thy mercy from me,
>   let thy steadfast love and thy faithfulness
>   ever preserve me!
> 12 For evils have encompassed me
>   without number;

[32] Cf. above, p. 52, n. 12.

my iniquities have overtaken me,
    till I cannot see;
they are more than the hairs of my head
    my heart fails me. (Ps 40:11-13)

9 I say to God, my rock:
    "Why has thou forgotten me?
Why go I mourning
    because of the oppression of the enemy?"
10 As with a deadly wound in my body,
    my adversaries taunt me,
while they say to me continually,
    "Where is your God?"
11 Why are you cast down, O my soul,
    and why are you so disquieted
        within me? (Ps 42:9-11)

43 Vindicate me, O God, and
    defend my cause against an ungodly people;
from deceitful and unjust men
    deliver me!
2 For thou art the God in whom I take refuge;
    why hast thou cast me off?
Why go I mourning
    because of the oppression of the enemy?

5 Why are you cast down, O my soul,
    and why are you so disquieted
        within me? (Ps 43: 1-2,5)

4 My heart is in anguish within me,
    the terrors of death have fallen
        upon me.
5 Fear and trembling come upon me,
    and horror overwhelms me.
6 And I say, "O that I had wings like
    a dove!
    I would fly away and be at rest;
7 yea, I would wander afar,
    I would lodge in the wilderness,

⁸ I would haste to find me a shelter
       from the raging wind and tempest."
       (Ps 55:4-8)

61 Hear my cry, O God,
       listen to my prayer;
² from the end of the earth I call to thee,
       when my heart is faint.
  Lead thou me
       to the rock that is higher than I;
³ for thou art my refuge,
       a strong tower against the enemy. (Ps 61:1-3)

³ The snares of death encompassed me;
       the pangs of Sheol laid hold on me;
       I suffered distress and anguish.
⁴ Then I called on the name of the Lord:
       "O Lord, I beseech thee, save
         my life!" (Ps 116:3-4)

It is unlikely that Mark (or the tradition before him) relied directly on any specific psalm text. The lament prayer was a well-known and classic prayer form of the Hebrew Scriptures. Surprisingly, the passion tradition is the sole place in the New Testament where this type of prayer is retained.[33]

The intensity of Jesus' anguish is directly stated in verse 34: "My soul is very sorrowful, even to death." The phrase "very sorrowful" repeats that found in the laments of Psalms 42:6,11, and 43:5. There is no hint in the text that Jesus' distress is caused by awareness of the sin of the world, as some Christian interpreters have suggested. Such pious reflection, in fact, tends to blunt the force of Mark's narrative. The evangelist presents Jesus as an example of biblical faith, a tormented child of God in love with life and fearful of death, without support except for the bedrock of God's fidelity. As the power of death begins to sweep over Jesus,

---

[33] On the theology of the lament and its use in the passion narratives, see P. D. Miller, Jr., "Trouble and Woe: Interpreting Biblical Laments," *Interpretation* 37 (1983), 32-45.

he warns his disciples to "remain" with him and to "stay awake" (v.34).

Jesus separates himself a short distance from the three disciples and as further sign of the intensity of his anguish casts himself on the ground in prayer. Mark first sums up the point of Jesus' prayer (14:35) and then quotes its content (14:36). The mood of the lament continues, with Jesus pleading that if it is possible, the hour might pass from him. The source of Jesus' anguish is the specter of imminent death.[34] Jesus who had expended his energy in healing bodies and casting out evil, who had cleansed the leper and raised Jairus' daughter from the grip of death, was now himself about to have his body broken and his spirit caught in the vice of ultimate evil. And so he prays for deliverance, as believers had done before in the wrenching laments of Israel.

The words of the prayer harmonize with the spirit of Jesus as Mark has presented him in the Gospel: "*Abba*, Father, all things are possible to you; remove this cup from me; yet not what I will but what you will."

Twice before Mark had noted Jesus alone at prayer (cf. 1:35; 6:46) but only now in the stillpoint of the Passion does the reader share in the content of that awesome communion between the Son of Man and the God for whom he lived. The address is terse and poignant: *Abba*! The word is Aramaic, a diminutive form of *ab*, or "father," used as an affectionate and reverential address by the Jewish child or adult for their parent. Mark immediately translates the term (*ho pater*, "father") for his Greek-speaking readers. The retention of the Aramaic suggests that Mark taps into an ancient tradition about Jesus' habitual prayer form, one indicating the unique bond between Jesus and the God of Israel.[35] Paul, too, shows he is aware of this tradition. As the

---

[34] O. Cullmann makes this point in his interesting comparison between Jesus and Socrates. Jesus, the Jew, recoils from death as an enemy while Socrates, the Greek, longs for immortality and thus welcomes death as a friend. Cf. "Immortality of the Soul or Resurrection of the Dead?" in K. Stendahl (ed.), *Immortality and Resurrection* (New York: MacMillan, 1965), 207-17.

[35] The direct address of God in prayer with the intimate term "Abba" is rare, if not unique, in what we know of first century Jewish piety. It therefore suggests the

apostle declares in Romans, to cry out "*Abba!*" Father!" in prayer is the heritage of the Christian, a gift of the Spirit signifying that one is a child of God released from the bondage of fear (see Rom 8:15-17; also Gal 4:6). That Jesus was God's beloved Son had been majestically proclaimed before in Mark's Gospel. At the Jordan, as Jesus had broken out of the waters of his baptism, a voice from the open heavens had proclaimed: "You are my beloved Son, with you I am well pleased" (1:10-11). On the mountain of transfiguration, as the journey toward Jerusalem was beginning, the voice had thundered again out of the overshadowing cloud: "This is my beloved Son..." (9:7). The demons, who felt the lash of Jesus' power breaking their grip on humanity had also acclaimed him as "Son of the Most High God" (5:7; cf. a similar text in 3:11 and 1:24). Now the communion between Father and Son is acclaimed by Jesus himself, not in the swirl of epiphany, or in the homage of the supernatural, but in the stark fear of approaching death.

The connotation of the term *Abba* is not only a note of affectionate intimacy, but also of reverence.[36] This is reflected in the phrase, "all things are possible to you" which reveals a basic sinew of biblical faith. Jesus' words are not the statement of an abstract dogmatic principle about God's sovereignty but express a profound conviction flowing from experience that the God of Israel holds all life in his hands. Such faith had characterized all of Jesus' teaching in Mark's Gospel. The key metaphor of Jesus' ministry — the advent of God's rule (1:14-15) — presupposed the power of God to transform and renew Israel. The seed metaphors in the parables had compared God's rule to an irrepressible harvest (4:20,28) or a tiny mustard seed that explodes into a huge

intense piety of Jesus. On the significance of this prayer form, cf. J. Jeremias, *The Prayers of Jesus* (Philadelphia: Fortress, 1978), 11-65; J. Dunn, *Jesus and the Spirit* (Philadelphia: Westminster, 1975), 21-40; M. Hengel, *The Son of God* (Philadelphia: Fortress, 1976), 63; D. Senior, *Jesus: A Gospel Portrait* (Dayton: Pflaum, 1975), 87-98. E. Schillebeeckx, *Jesus: An Experiment in Christology* (New York: Seabury, 1979), 256-71.

[36] E. Schillebeeckx, *Jesus*, 262-63.

tree (4:32), or a seed apparently smothered in the earth, which surprises its planter by bursting into bloom (4:26-29). In each instance the staggering power of God is assumed. Jesus, too, had instructed the father of a stricken son that "all things are possible to the one who believes" (9:23). When the disciples were thunderstruck at his teaching on renouncing wealth, Jesus had reassured them, "all things are possible with God" (10:27).[37] In Jerusalem on the way back from the temple, the Marcan Jesus had instructed his disciples:

> "[22]Have faith in God. [23]Truly, I say to you, whoever says to this mountain, 'Be taken up and cast into the sea,' and does not doubt in his heart, but believes that what he says will come to pass, it will be done for him. [24]Therefore I tell you, whatever you ask in prayer, believe that you have received it, and it will be yours." (11:22-24)

When the Sadducees attempted to subdue Jesus by arguing the absurdity of resurrection, he openly challenged them: "...you know neither the scripture nor the *power* of God" (12:24).

Mark, therefore, presents Jesus as following through on his own teaching; he prays as he had lived and preached, one who, indeed, knew "the power of God" and entrusted his life and future to it.

The remainder of the prayer comes to the very heart of the lament. About to be snared in the trap of death, Jesus prays for deliverance: "remove this cup from me" (14:36b). In the context of Mark's entire Gospel it is a bold and shocking prayer. From the encounter at Caesarea Philippi to the celebration of his final Passover, Jesus had clearly stated that the destiny of the Son of Man was to "drink the cup," to

---

[37] In two texts just cited, the language is nearly identical to the words of the Gethsemane prayer:
9:23 "all things are possible to the one who believes" (*panta dunata tō pisteuonti*)
10:27 "all things are possible with God" (*panta...dunata para tō theō*)
14:36 "all things are possible to you" (*panta dunata soi*).

lay down his life for the many. When James and John had swaggered forward to seek places of power with him, he had challenged them: "Are you able to drink the cup that I drink?" (10:38). Now in the moment of crisis Mark depicts Jesus as pleading with the God who can do all things to *take away* the cup destined for the Son of Man. The raw honesty and stunning humanness of such a prayer is totally within the great tradition of the Jewish lament. Prayer is not to be ideal, fully controlled, or strained with politeness. In a rush of emotion, complaint, and even recrimination, the believers pour out their hearts to God.

The reader, of course, is not in doubt about the spirit of Jesus' prayer. The terse conclusion — "Yet not what I will, but what you will" — taps the deepest current of Jesus' life as presented by Mark. Some interpreters draw the conclusion that Mark must have been aware of the tradition of the Lord's prayer since this portion of Jesus' prayer is so similar (cf. Mt 6:10).[38] While this is quite possible, we should also note that the evangelist had already made dedication to God's will a hallmark of Jesus. In the remarkable account of Jesus and his family, singular commitment to the will of God had been unforgettably proclaimed. Jesus' mother and brothers who had come after him to take him home, fearing for his sanity (see 3:20-21), stand outside the house where he is teaching (3:31-35). When the crowd tells Jesus that his family seeks him, he looks at the circle of followers *inside* the house and says: "Here are my mother and brother! Whoever does the will of God is my brother, and sister, and mother" (3:35). Kinship with Jesus would be based not on blood lines but on dedication to the will of God. When the scribes in Jerusalem asked him about the greatest commandment of the law, Jesus had recited the *shema*, the great creed of Israel taken from Deuteronomy 6:4 — "Hear O Israel. The Lord our God, the Lord is one; and you shall love the Lord your God with all your heart, and with all your soul, and with all your mind, and with all your

---

[38] See the discussion in D. Stanley, *Jesus in Gethsemane*, 125, 135-37; H. Kruse, "'Pater Noster' et Passio Christi," *Verbum Domini* 46 (1968), 3-39; S. von Tilborg, "A Form Criticism of the Lord's Prayer," *Novum Testamentum* 14 (1972), 94-105.

strength" (12:28-30).

Mark leaves no doubt about the fierce commitment of Jesus, the beloved Son, to the will of God. The Gethsemane prayer is a lament but through the choked voice of the prayer is expressed the tenacious dedication of Jesus to his mission of compassion and service to the point of death (10:45). The Son of Man would drink the cup because in the baffling paradox of God's will, this was the way.

Mark does not provide any more content to Jesus' Gethsemane prayer than the terse and powerful words of v.36. The prayer is repeated three times: in v.39 Jesus goes away and prays "saying the same words;" in v.41 we are told he *returns* from prayer a "third time." The efficacious pattern of threefold prayer was a stock theme in Judaism, but, as we shall see, Mark's interest is elsewhere. Once the prayer of Jesus has been eloquently stated, Mark's attention turns from christology to its accompanying theme of discipleship.

The Sleep of the Disciples

Throughout the Gospel, the many instances of the disciples' incomprehension and their repeated failure to accept Jesus' instructions on the Passion have braced the reader for the collapse of their discipleship.[39] Jesus' predictions of their desertion and Peter's denial in the immediately preceding Passover scenes had made the expectation acute. Now the disciples' astounding reactions in Gethsemane will complete the scenario.

Before beginning his own intense prayer Jesus had warned the three disciples to "stay awake" (14:34). That command recalls the conclusion of the final discourse that had taken place on this same mountain before the beginning of the passion story: "And what I say to you I say to all: Stay awake" (13:37; cf. all of 13:32-37). Staying awake in watchful alertness was the stance the community must take as it carried out its mission to the world in the midst of opposition and threat (13:9-12). Until the Son of Man would come

[39] Cf. our discussion of this motif in Mark, above, pp. 31-35.

in triumph to gather the elect, the disciples must be sober and alert. Mark now draws that eschatological atmosphere into the Passion story. Instead of being awake in prayer, the disciples repeatedly sink into the torpor of sleep. After his first prayer Jesus returns to the disciples and confronts Peter: "Simon, are you asleep? Could you not watch (*gregoresai*, this word for "stay awake" or "watch" is used throughout this portion of the text) one hour?" (14:37). After each of Jesus' prayers the results will be the same: they fail by sleeping instead of watching (cf. 14:40,41). The threefold indictment of the disciples' sleep is in stark contrast to Jesus' repeated prayer.

Jesus' remarks add further insight into the meaning of the scene. They are to "watch and pray" to avoid entering "into the test" (14:38). The term *perasmos* or "test" recalls one of the opening scenes of the Gospel where Jesus was driven into the desert by the Spirit to confront Satan, the power of evil (cf. 1:12-13). Here in the wilderness, the place of Israel's own desert trial, the Son of God would be "tested" (*peirazomenos*, the identical verb as in 14:41). This brilliant, wordless scene serves as prelude to and preview of Jesus' entire ministry.[40] The struggle with Satan in the mythical setting of the desert would be repeated in the human arena of Galilee as Jesus liberated broken bodies and tortured minds from the grip of evil.

By Jesus' warning to the disciples in Gethsemane about the impending "test," Mark implies that the passion is the final struggle with evil. By defeating death Jesus will triumph over the ultimate evil that grips creation. It is a vicious contest that only the Spirit-filled Son of God can win; the disciples must pray not to be engulfed by it. The Gospel's assessment of the power of evil is sober and realistic. Mark conceives of the passion not simply as Jesus of Nazareth's encounter with death, but from the perspective of full resurrection faith, as a story of humanity's own struggle with the power of evil in the world.[41]

[40] Cf. J. M. Robinson, *The Problem of History in Mark and Other Marcan Studies* (Philadelphia: Fortress, 1982), 69-80.
[41] On this cf. above, pp. 37-39.

But the disciples' sleep remains impenetrable: "The spirit is willing but the flesh is weak" (14:38). That cleavage reflects a basic biblical anthropology, one that emerges in Paul and other New Testament writings as well.[42] The dividing line is not that between "soul" and "body," but between basic orientations within the human person. The "spirit" is the transcendent dimension, responsive to God; while the "flesh" is the mortal, limited, and egotistical tendency of the human person. To be spirit-dominated was, in Pauline thought, the outcome of redemption (see, for example, Romans 8:1-17). A similar pattern seems to be expressed here. The "spirit is willing" (the phrase echoes Psalm 51:12) and catches God's lure of grace, but the flesh is inert, unable to respond to the moment. The disciples at this point are flesh-dominated and thus they sleep — "They did not know how to respond" (14:40), words that echo the incomprehension of Peter before the epiphany of a transfigured Jesus (cf. 9:6).

The scene climbs to its crescendo in vs. 41-42. After finding them asleep for the third time, Jesus curtly states: "enough".[43] The passion now begins. By the statement which closes the scene Mark seems to envisage the convergence of three fateful forces:

—"the hour has come"
—"The Son of Man is handed over"
—"the betrayer is at hand."

The "hour" is not merely one moment in time but connotes that critical and definitive hour when the salvation of the world would be decided.[44] It is to this hour, the "handing

---

[42] Cf. H. W. Wolff, *Anthropology of the Old Testament* (Philadelphia: Fortress, 1974), 26-39; on Paul's anthropology, cf. J. Fitzmyer, "Pauline Theology," in *The Jerome Biblical Commentary* (Englewood Cliffs, NJ: Prentice-Hall, 1968) Vol. II, 820-21.

[43] The Greek word translated as "enough" is *apechei*, an extremely obscure expression. Translating it as "enough," in the sense of ending the discussion between Jesus and the disciples, is one among several possible interpretations.

[44] The same term is used in the final discourse of chapter 13 to refer to the endtime: "But of that day or that *hour* no one knows, not even the angels in heaven, nor the Son but only the Father" (13:32). In 13:11 the disciples are told not to be anxious when they are brought to trial in the pursuit of their mission, "but say whatever is given you in that *hour*, for it is not you who speak, but the Holy Spirit."

over," that the Son of Man had moved like an arrow towards its target. And Judas, too, had sought this moment since the tragic barter with the priests had been sealed (14:11). Jesus' purposeful command — "rise, let us go" (v.42) — demonstrates that, despite the loss of freedom about to engulf Jesus, his death is no tragic imposition but an act of service freely chosen. Those deliberate words of Jesus, cutting across the torpor of the disciples, also illumine a basic purpose of the Gethsemane tradition. The Christian reader could not fail to notice the impact of prayer on Jesus. Communion with his *Abba* had soothed Jesus' lament and steeled him for the crisis. The disciples who failed to pray are overwhelmed with fear and will flee.

B) THE ARREST (14:43-52)

Jesus' declaration that the betrayer is at hand (14:42) is immediately confirmed. Mark fuses his account of the arrest directly on to the Gethsemane story: "and immediately while he was still speaking..." (v.43). Despite their plots, Jesus' opponents have not taken him by surprise.

The moment of the arrest is one of the most important in the entire passion narrative. The passion predictions that have prepared the reader for Jesus' sufferings from chapter 8 on point to the "handing over" or the moment of arrest when the Son of Man was delivered to his enemies (cf. 8:31; 9:31; 10:33). The focus of the passion tradition on the arrest, as much as on the trial or the death itself, is validated by other martyrdom accounts, including those of our own day. The violent pounding of fists on the door in the middle of the night, the terror of those snatched into a fleeing car on a city street — these are images that are told time and time again about modern martyrs. The arrest clutches our attention because here is where freedom is violated and the forces of good and evil stand face to face. In the moment of arrest the courage and integrity of the martyrs, as well as the viciousness of their captors, are on public display. Often the events following the arrest are unknown, or follow their inevitable sequence to death. In such cases the arrest story alone stands as the martyrdom account. The arrest scene of Jesus reflects some of those perennial characteristics. Although the arrest has been envisioned early in the Gospel and was immediately prepared for by the reporting of the plot (14:1-2), betrayal (14:10-11) and Jesus' predictions (14:17-21, 26-31, 42), Mark's description is understated, with a minimum of theological elaboration. It is as if the stark horror of the events speaks itself.

The scene opens with Judas' leading a crowd of people apparently gathered by the Sanhedrin (14:43). The tragedy of the moment strikes home: Judas is explicitly identified as "one of the twelve," as he had been in Jesus' prediction of betrayal (14:20; cf. also 14:10; 3:19). His "opportune moment" (14:11) has arrived and the abandonment of his discipleship is complete because now he is in full communion with those who are seeking to destroy Jesus. The opponents are described as the "chief priests and the scribes and the elders," the full range of the Jerusalem establishment that had stalked Jesus since his action in the temple (cf. 11:27).[45] The "crowd" they send is armed with swords and clubs, a detail which gives the whole scene an atmosphere of violence.

The sign of betrayal is a kiss (14:44-45). The evangelist is terse: Judas greets Jesus with the address "Rabbi" and kisses him.[46] Thereby Mark brings to a chilling climax the motif of friendship betrayal he had orchestrated throughout the opening scenes (see, above, 14:17-21). Jesus is, indeed, the Just One of Israel abandoned and tormented by those he loved. The kiss could be a normal sign of greeting between master and disciple but Judas' intent makes it sinister, transforming a sign of love into a signal for death. Treacherous use of a kiss is found in some vivid stories of the Bible. Absalom had ingratiated himself with those coming to David's court by kissing them rather than accepting their sign

[45] Previously, Jesus' Jerusalem opponents had been listed as the "chief priests and scribes" (11:18; 14:1) or the "chief priests" (14:10).

[46] Mark had used the term "rabbi" as a respectful address for Jesus earlier in the Gospel: cf. 9:5; 10:51; 11:21.

of obeisance (II Sam 15:5). Joab, with a sword hidden in his right hand, disembowels Amara, catching him off guard by seizing his beard and kissing him (II Sam 20:8-10). The wry comment of Proverbs has the last word: "Faithful are the words of a friend; profuse are the kisses of an enemy" (Proverb 27:6).[47] The sinister trigger of the kiss moves the armed band to seize Jesus (14:46). In stark, unelaborated words Mark reports the awesome moment of the "handing over." A bizarre incident accompanies the arrest, one that heightens the atmosphere of brutality. "One of those who stood by" draws a sword and cuts off the ear of the high priest's slave (14:47). All of the other evangelists assume that the swordbearer was a disciple (John is most specific, identifying the disciple as Peter and the slave as Malchus; see John 18:10-11) and use the incident as a teaching moment in which Jesus rejects the use of violence.[48] In Mark the scene is quite different. Read without the interpretation given by the other evangelists it could well be that the one who strikes with the sword is *not* a disciple but one of the *crowd* which comes to arrest Jesus.[49] The attacker is not identified as a "disciple" or as one of those "with" (Mt 26:51) or "around" (Lk 22:49) Jesus; he is "one of those who stood by."[50] Since in Mark's account Jesus' response is directed to the *crowd* (the "them" of 14:48-49) and not to his disciples (as it is in the other evangelists), one could assume that the "bystander" belongs to the hostile mob not to Jesus' own company. The wounding of the High Priest's slave would not be

---

[47] On the kiss as an act of betrayal in Jewish and other ancient literature, cf. R. Pesch, *Das Markusevangelium*, II, 400 and G. Stahlin in G. Kittel (ed.), *Theological Dictionary of the New Testament*, IX, 140-141.

[48] Cf. Mt. 26:52-53; Lk. 22:51; John 18:10-11 (also 19:36).

[49] Cf., for example, R. Pesch, *Das Markusevangelium,* II, 400-01 and L. Schenke, *Der gekreuzigte Christus* (Stuttgarter Bibelstudien 68; Stuttgart: KBW, 1974), 118-20. E. Schweizer suggests it was not one of those coming to arrest Jesus but a "sympathetic onlooker"; cf. *The Good News According to Mark* (Atlanta: John Knox Press, 1970), 318.

[50] This same term is used elsewhere in the passion story to refer to a surrounding crowd as in 14:69-70 (the bystanders who accuse Peter of being a Galilean) and 15:35 (those standing around the cross, some of whom mockingly misinterpret Jesus' final prayer).

a deliberate attack on the slave (who presumably was one of those come to arrest Jesus, too) but an accident resulting from the mob scene. Thus as one of the mob draws his sword he accidently slashes the High Priest's servant. The initiative now swings to Jesus as he addresses his captors (14:48-49). Whereas the other Gospels use the sword incident for Jesus' instruction on violence, Mark concentrates solely on the contrast between Jesus' own clear integrity and the devious brutality of his opponents. They have come out, at night, on the eve of the Passover, to capture Jesus with swords and clubs as if he were a robber. But Jesus taught openly in the temple, in the light of day, and they did not seize him. Jesus' fearless challenge to his captors recalls the temple scenes of chapters 11-12 where his final teaching had taken place. His wisdom had stunned his opponents into silence (12:34) and they wanted to arrest him then but feared the crowds (11:18; 12:12; 14:2). Jesus' words in the garden expose the fear which had attempted to mask itself with weapons and the cover of darkness.

Note that this vivid contrast between Jesus' way and that of his opponents is an implicit foundation for the condemnation of the sword that the other evangelists introduce into this scene. Jesus' power does not lie with the power of coercion and brutal force. That critique of worldly power will come to the surface in Mark's presentation of the trial of Jesus, with its parody of the trappings of kingship.

"But let the scriptures be fulfilled." (14:49) Jesus' words point to the ultimate meaning of this terrible moment. The forces of violence, despite the fact that they hold Jesus in their grip, are not in control. Jesus' handing over to the cross will paradoxically fulfill God's purpose. The term "scriptures" used here refers not to some specific texts in which the moment of arrest is foreshadowed but to the entire salvific intent of God which the early church saw woven into the Bible. Jesus was the servant who gave his life in ransom for the many, the Son of Man destined to triumph through the paradox of humiliation and death, the Just One betrayed by his friends but vindicated by a faithful God, the Messiah who in spite of rejection and death would drink the triumphant wine of the King's banquet. In all of these biblical images, the early community read the mystery of God's way.[51] Jesus' words seem to allow the arrest to go forward and in so doing another frightful chapter of the passion story comes to pass: the disciples abandon Jesus (14:50). Jesus' prediction at the Passover meal comes true (cf. 14:27). Mark's description is both stark and poignant. The literal wording of the Greek text catches the abject failure of Jesus' followers: "and leaving him they fled, all of them." The word "all" (*pantes*) echoes the emphasis of Jesus' prophetic words — "all" (*pantes*) of you will be scandalized in me."

This scene of mob violence concludes with a haunting and bizarre epilogue (14:51-52). As the disciples flee into the night, the crowd lunges at a "young man" who had been following Jesus. He had been garbed only in a linen cloth and as the crowd lays hands on him he slips out of his garment and flees naked. Some interpreters consider this a symbolic incident (it is unique to Mark). The term used to describe the "young man" (*neaniskos*) is identical with that used in 16:5 to describe the figure who greets the women at the empty tomb. And the *sindona* or "linen cloth" covering the young man is the same word used to describe Jesus' burial cloth in 15:46. Therefore some have suggested that this strange incident in the garden is a symbolic prelude to the resurrection story: as Jesus is arrested the narrative flashes ahead to the empty tomb story. Jesus will ultimately escape from the clutches of death in resurrection, shedding his burial garments as the young man does in the garden. Others prefer to see a historical incident or the traces of some exotic ritual or motif whose original meaning is lost in the text.[52]

While the symbolic meaning or the fact of a historical

---

[51] On the use of the Old Testament in the Passion narratives, cf. D. Moo, *The Old Testament in the Gospel Passion Narratives* (Sheffield, England: The Almond Press, 1983), and B. Lindars, *New Testament Apologetic: The Doctrinal Significance of the Old Testament Quotations* (Philadelphia: Westminster, 1961), 75-137.

[52] Cf. a review of these various interpretations in H. Fleddermann, "The Flight of a Naked Young Man (Mark 14:51-52)," *The Catholic Biblical Quarterly* 41 (1979), 412-17. Fleddermann's proposal that through this incident Mark emphasizes the panic and fear of the disciples seems most plausible.

reminiscence cannot be ruled out, there may be a simpler explanation for the function of this incident in Mark's narrative. The headlong flight of the young follower of Jesus, bolting in panic and leaving his clothes behind, not only fits the terrible confusion of the mob scene (and the almost comic violence of the sword incident) but it reenforces the impression of a complete breakdown on the part of the disciples. Their fear totally overwhelms their allegiance to Jesus. The disciples who had "left all" to follow Jesus (cf. 1:18,20; 10:28) now, in the crisis of the passion, abandon everything — their allegiance, their word, even their clothing — to flee from him. Once again the Christian reader is compelled to ponder the tenacity of his or her own commitment.

IV. The Trial Before the Sanhedrin: Confession and Denial (Mark 14:53-72)

The passion story now moves to a major change of setting. From Gethsemane where Jesus was arrested the scene now shifts to the court of the High Priest where he will be tried by the Sanhedrin. Mark keeps both Jesus and his lingering disciple Peter in view (14:53-54). Around them will swirl the events that dominate this section: Jesus' confession that he is the "Christ, the Son of the Blessed" and the exalted Son of Man (14:55-64), and Peter's vehement denial that he is a disciple (14:66-72).

> [53]And they led Jesus to the high priest; and all the chief priests and the elders and the scribes were assembled. [54]And Peter had followed him at a distance, right into the courtyard of the high priest; and he was sitting with the guards, and warming himself at the fire. [55]Now the chief priests and their whole council sought testimony against Jesus to put him to death; but they found none. [56]For many bore false witness against him, and their witness did not agree. [57]And some stood up and

bore false witness against him, saying, [58]"We heard him say, 'I will destroy this temple that is made with hands, and in three days I will build another, not made with hands.'" [59]Yet not even so did their testimony agree. [60]And the high priest stood up in the midst, and asked Jesus, "Have you no answer to make? What is it that these men testify against you? [61]But he was silent and made no answer. Again the high priest asked him, "Are you the Christ, the Son of the Blessed?" [62]And Jesus said, "I am; and you will see the Son of Man seated at the right hand of Power, and coming with the clouds of heaven." [63]And the high priest tore his garments, and said, "Why do we still need witnesses? [64]You have heard his blasphemy. What is your decision?" And they all condemned him as deserving death. [65]And some began to spit on him, and to cover his face, and to strike him, saying to him, "Prophesy!" And the guards received him with blows.

[66]And as Peter was below in the courtyard, one of the maids of the high priest came; [67]and seeing Peter warming himself, she looked at him, and said, "You also were with the Nazarene, Jesus." [68]But he denied it, saying, "I neither know nor understand what you mean." And he went out into the gateway. [69]And the maid saw him, and began again to say to the bystanders, "This man is one of them." [70]But again he denied it. And after a little while again the bystanders said to Peter, "Certainly you are one of them; for you are a Galilean." [71]But he began to invoke a curse on himself and to swear, "I do not know this man of whom you speak." [72]And immediately the cock crowed a second time. And Peter remembered how Jesus had said to him, "Before the cock crows twice, you will deny me three times." And he broke down and wept. (14:53-72)

A) JESUS AND PETER (14:53-54)

Mark sets the scene with skill and care. The crowd who had seized Jesus brings him to the residence of the High Priest, probably located on the high ground northwest of the temple area, which later would be known as "Christian

Zion."[53] Here the full Sanhedrin has assembled: the chief priests, the elders and the scribes (cf. 14:43, the same group that had sent Judas and the crowd to arrest Jesus). The Sanhedrin was a council with ruling power over religious and civil matters. Its members were the ranking leaders of the Jewish community: the priests, the elders — most of whom were drawn from the aristocratic Sadducee party — and the educated scribes who included lawyers and theologians, some of whom would have been Pharisees. The Sanhedrin was led by the high priest, Caiaphas, who served as High Priest from A.D. 18-37, is not named by Mark (compare Mt. 26:57). The frustrated attempts of the leaders to strike at Jesus could now be carried out. He was face to face with his enemies, on their terms.

Peter's presence on the margin of the trial will serve Mark's consistent dual focus on christology and discipleship (14:54-55). Even though the flight of "all" the disciples had been described at the end of the arrest scene (14:50), the reader had been prepared for Peter's exception. After the Passover meal, the disciple who had been the first called by Jesus (1:16-18) had sworn that "even if they all fall away, I will not" (14:29). Even when Jesus had predicted his denial, Peter had insisted: "If I must die with you, I will not deny you" (14:31). Two contradictory promises — Jesus' and Peter's — hang in the air, and now the reader will see the outcome.

To this point Peter's pledge of loyalty still holds: he follows Jesus into the High Priest's courtyard. But the eventual result may already be hinted at: Peter follows "at a distance." In Psalm 38 the Just One laments that "my friends and companions stand aloof from my plague, and my kinsmen stand *afar off*"(the same Greek phrase is used in the Greek version of Psalm 38:12 as in Mark 14:54. Peter sits down with guards and warms himself at the fire (14:54).) The evangelist deftly lays out the scene. The focus will swing first

---

[53] On this point, see J. Wilkinson, *Jerusalem As Jesus Knew It: Archaeology as Evidence* (London: Thames and Hudson, 1978) 131-37.

to Jesus standing before his captives (14:55-65) and then
move back outside to Peter by the fire (14:66-72). Thereby
the cowardice and denial of Peter under the questioning of
servants frames the forceful confession of Jesus as he is
interrogated by the High Priest and the Sanhedrin.

B) THE CONFESSION BEFORE THE SANHEDRIN (14:55-65)

This important passage raises a number of historical and
theological questions. Mark presents the scene as a "trial."
Jesus is brought before the full Sanhedrin. Testimony is
directed against him and he is formally interrogated by the
High Priest. On the basis of his answer, he is condemned to
death for blasphemy. However, many scholars would argue
that this procedure could not have been a trial. Later Jewish
texts expressly forbade many of the procedures used in the
process described by Mark: 1) It was held on the Passover
whereas trials on the Sabbath and feastdays were forbidden;
2) It was held at night and in the house of the High Priest
(rather than in the official court of the Sanhedrin) — both
circumstances illegal; 3) The sentence of death followed
immediately after the proceedings whereas the law
demanded that a lapse of time intervene; 4) The testimony of
witnesses did not agree whereas the Law demanded scrupu-
lous agreement among witnesses; 5) Jesus was condemned
for blasphemy (14:64-65) but blasphemy referred to pro-
nouncing the divine name. Further complications come
from the fact that Jesus was crucified. What relationship
does this imply between the action of the Sanhedrin and
Pilate's Roman court? Did the Sanhedrin have the right to
capital punishment? Or did they have to consign such cases
to Roman jurisdiction?[54]

Attempts to solve these historical issues are probably
doomed to frustration. The sources which detail these Jew-

[54] Cf. the discussion in J. Donahue, "Temple, Trial, and Royal Christology (Mark 14:53-65)," in W. Kelber (ed.), *The Passion in Mark*, 61-2, and the literature cited above, p. 41, n.2.

ish legal procedures date from a much later period and we cannot be sure if they were in effect in the very different atmosphere prior to A.D.70. In addition we cannot assume that our conception of the strict canons of legality in judicial procedures match the concerns of the first century.

Some authors accept the Marcan account as a basically accurate rendition of events, that is, a trial by the Sanhedrin and then transfer to the court of Pilate to secure capital punishment. The unusual circumstances of the trial before the Sanhedrin as described by Mark could either make it illegal, if the regulations known from later sources were already in effect in Jesus' day, or if different procedures were allowed prior to A.D.70, the proceedings may have been legal.

Other scholars question whether a Jewish trial took place at all. Some would hold that the Romans were solely responsible for Jesus' execution and the account of a Jewish trial was created by the early church both to downplay Roman initiatives against Jesus — thereby assuring the Roman world that Jesus was innocent of the charge of sedition — and to blame the Jews for the rejection of the Messiah.[55]

However, many scholars question whether the Gospels have so distorted the record and suggest that the Jewish "trial" may actually have been an *interrogation* of Jesus and a strategy session in preparation for bringing him before Pilate where a formal trial would take place. Thus some involvement in Jesus' condemnation on the part of some Jewish leaders would have taken place, but this would not have included formal sentencing by the Sanhedrin. Later tradition — perhaps under the influence of the Roman trial scene — would have amplified what may have been an interrogation or hearing into a full blown trial account.[56]

This whole debate is an important one because it takes place against the backdrop of Christian anti-Semitism. The

55 This is the general thesis of S. Brandon, *The Trial of Jesus of Nazareth* (London: Paladin, 1968).

56 Cf. G. Sloyan's careful conclusions on this point in *Jesus on Trial*, 126-34.

condemnation of Jesus by the Sanhedrin and the alleged illegality of the proceedings have been used as one of the excuses for vicious slander of the Jewish people as a whole. Even if historical facts were to reveal that Jesus had been tried by the Sanhedrin, legally or illegally, this would be no cause for condemnation of the Jewish people and would therefore remain a condemnable misuse of the Gospel.

In any case, our analysis of Mark's text will not solve the historical riddles. Mark's purpose is neither to offer a detailed historical account nor to indict the Jewish leaders. His intentions are primarily theological. In the paradoxical setting of a helpless prisoner before his accusers, the Gospel will boldly proclaim Jesus as the Messiah. For this purpose, Mark will employ motifs carefully orchestrated throughout his Gospel.

The evangelist portrays the entire proceeding as an effort to muster false witness against the innocent Jesus (14:55,56,59). In so doing the mantle of the suffering Just One is again cast around Jesus' shoulders. The psalmist had exclaimed: "Give me not up to the will of my adversaries; for false witnesses have arisen against me, and they breathe out violence" (Psalm 27:12). A similar lament is found in Psalm 35:11-12: "Malicious witnesses rise up; they ask me of things I know not. They requite me evil for good; my soul is forlorn." The attacks on the "Just One" by false witnesses as well as the abandonment by friends are all pieces of this motif which appears frequently in the Psalms and comes to potent expression in the Book of Wisdom (see, especially 2:12-20; 5:1-5). Jesus *is* the Just One abandoned by humanity, tested in his fidelity but vindicated by God.

This fundamental interpretation of Jesus' death and resurrection was probably an important motif of the passion tradition long before Mark's formulation of the story. Although he does retain this theme, Mark's own special interests in this scene seem to lie in a related, but different set of metaphors: the new temple (14:58) and the brace of christological titles that will be applied to Jesus (14:61-62).

The Temple not made by hands

One of the major accusations against Jesus is his alleged threats against the Jerusalem temple: "We heard him say, 'I will destroy this temple that is made with hands, and in three days I will build another, not made with hands' " (14:58). A similar accusation will be hurled at Jesus by those who taunt him at the cross: "Aha! You who would destroy this temple in three days, save yourself, and come down from the cross" (15:30).

At first blush it might seem that the evangelist brands this as *false* testimony and, therefore, as not stating anything true or significant about Jesus. Those who stand up to make the accusation are said to "bear false witness against him" (14:57). In 14:59 Mark notes that "their testimony did not agree." However there are good reasons to believe that some irony may be at work here. Even though Jesus' enemies intend false witness and their testimony is not in agreement (thus invalidating it according to Jewish Law), the *reader* is aware of a deeper truth expressed unwittingly by the accusers.

First of all Mark has prepared for this moment by his description of Jesus' activity in the temple (chapters 11-13). As we noted in discussing those passages, Mark presents Jesus as condemning the old temple (11:15-19; see also 13:2) and preparing the way for a "new temple", one that will be "a house of prayer for all nations" (11:17), for which the Risen Christ himself will be the cornerstone (12:10-11). This temple is the community itself, created through the death and resurrection of Jesus. The old temple, representative of the false values exemplified by Jesus' opponents, will be no more.[57]

The accusation in 14:58 restates the theme which was implicit in the earlier chapters. Mark heightens the irony by framing this key verse with references to the false accusers

[57] See our discussion of this motif above, pp. 24-28.

who mobilize against Jesus (cf. 14:57,59). Their malicious intent and confusion only intensifies the drama, as what they believe will count against Jesus serves to proclaim the bold truth about him. This happens at other places in the Gospel. The scribes challenge Jesus' right to forgive sins (2:7) and the mockers at the cross taunt Jesus with statements that the reader knows are profoundly true (cf. 15:31, "He saved others; he cannot save himself").[58]

Thus Jesus will destroy a temple made of hands and rebuild a new and spiritual temple in three days. This formulation expresses not the actual words of Jesus but Mark's interpretation of events in the light of the death and resurrection. At the moment of Jesus' death the temple veil is torn in two (15:38), a symbolic action proclaiming that the validity of the temple had come to an end. Now God's power and revelation stream from the Risen Christ and authentic worship is found in those who recognize this presence, that is, the Christian community represented by the Gentile centurion who confesses Jesus as Son of God (15:39).

The couplet "made by hands"/"not made by hands" is unique to Mark's Gospel. The Bible had characterized pagan gods as being "made by hands"; that is, of purely human origin (e.g. Psalm 115:4; Wisdom 13:10). Therefore, the dual phrases might imply that what was of human origin is now replaced by something of authentic divine origin (that is, "not made by hands"). But this seems an exceptionally negative statement about the Jerusalem temple, even by a Christian author. More likely the phrase points to the contrast between a physical structure ("made by hands") and the *spiritual* reality ("not made by hands") of the community as temple. The term "in three days," can simply mean "after a while" (see, for example, Hosea 6:2). But in view of the fact that Mark links the temple symbolism to the moment of Jesus' death, it is likely that the reference here connotes the resurrection, the third day on which Jesus was raised from the dead and the community reborn. A similar

---

[58] Cf. E. Best, *Discipleship in Mark*, 214; J. Donahue, "Temple, Trial, and Royal Christology," 67.

but not identical time indication is used in the passion predictions in reference to the resurrection (cf. 8:31; 9:31; 10:34).

The temple accusation takes on a special focus in the context of the trial before the Sanhedrin. Now the alleged saying of Jesus is more than a metaphorical reflection on the Christian community as the new and spiritual temple. It also points to Jesus' authority as the one who condemns the old temple and builds the new ("We heard *him* say, *I* will destroy... *I* will build..."). The question of Jesus' authority over the temple had arisen earlier in the Gospel. Immediately after his actions in the temple the "chief priests and the scribes and the elders" (significantly the full Sanhedrin who now accuse him in the trial) demanded of Jesus, "By what authority are you doing these things, or who gave you this authority to do them?" (11:27-28). Jesus refuses to answer their questions because his interrogators are insincere, their rejection of the message of the Baptist being proof (11:29-33). In the trial, too, Jesus will not respond to testimony whose intent is false (14:60-61).

But the reader of Mark's Gospel is in a different position. There is evidence that in the first century Jewish tradition did expect a purification or even a destruction of the temple to take place as part of the cataclysmic events of the final age. Some Jewish targums point to the Messiah as the one who would rebuild the temple but we cannot be certain how prevalent this expectation was in Jesus' day.[59] However, it does seem likely that Jesus' alleged threats against the temple first found their way into the passion story because they raised the issue of his claim to be Messiah.[60] For Mark the accusations of the false witnesses are ironically true: Jesus is the Messiah who enters Jerusalem to render judgment over the old temple and to announce a new order. It is quite

---

[59] Cf. the discussion in L. Gaston, *No Stone on Another, Studies in the Significance of the Fall of Jerusalem in the Synoptic Gospels* (Supplements to Novum Testamentum 23; Leiden: Brill, 1970), 147-154; D. Juel, *Messiah and Temple*, 169-209

[60] R. Pesch, for example, sees this as the basis of the charges originally brought against Jesus by his opponents; cf. *Das Markusevangelium*, II, 427-46.

possible that Mark writes after the fall of Jerusalem and the destruction of the temple, in which case he and his community interpreted those tragic events as the fulfillment of Jesus' prophetic judgment (cf. 13:2,14) and as confirmation of his messianic authority.

Christ, Son of God, Son of Man

Jesus remains silent when the High Priest asks him to respond to the false witness about the temple. That eloquent silence may be designed to invoke the memory of the Servant of Yahweh who remained silent as he bore the iniquity of the community:

> He was oppressed, and he was afflicted,
>> yet he opened not his mouth;
>> like a lamb that is led to the
>>   slaughter,
>> and like a sheep that before its
>>   shearers is dumb,
>> so he opened not his mouth. (Is 53:7)

That silence leads to the climactic point of the trial. The High Priest as leader of the Sanhedrin directs the key question to Jesus: "Are you the Christ, the Son of the Blessed?" (14:61). The answer is immediate: "I am; and you will see the Son of Man sitting at the right hand of Power, and coming with the clouds of heaven" (14:62). These are perhaps the most condensed christological statements in Mark and represent the culmination of motifs that run the length of the Gospel. In the setting of the passion, as never before, Jesus clearly accepts the threefold designation as Christ, Son of the Blessed (equivalent to Son of God) and Son of Man.

It may be helpful to review Mark's preparation for this moment. Throughout the Gospel Mark has asserted Jesus' identity as the Davidic Messiah, the royal figure expected to come as God's agent of salvation and renewal in the final days. That designation is given to him in the opening line or title of the Gospel: "The Beginning of the Gospel of Jesus *Christ*, the Son of God" (1:1). At Caesarea Philippi, Peter acclaims: "You are the Christ" (8:29). In 9:41 the disciples of Jesus are referred to as bearing "the name of Christ." *False* "christs" come claiming to be Jesus the exalted Son of Man, texts which indirectly reserve the title to Jesus (13:21,22). The taunts of the mockers at the crucifixion — "Let the Christ, the King of Israel, come down now from the cross... (15:32) — bear the same ironical confession of Jesus' true identity.

Mark also proclaims Jesus' Messiahship in other ways. Jesus' mission is summarized as inaugurating God's rule (1:14-15 *et passim*). He is solemnly designated as God's Son at the baptism in the Jordan, echoing the words enthroning the Davidic King, "I will tell of the decree of the Lord: He said to me, "You are my Son today I have begotten you" (Psalm 2:7; Mark 1:11). A similar acclamation comes at the transfiguration (9:7). The exorcisms and healings of Jesus recounted by Mark may also have been understood as the action of the Messiah.[61] The demons shrink in terror before him and address him as "Son of the Most High God" (5:7), another designation for the royal Messiah. Bartimaeus appeals to Jesus as "Son of David" at Jericho (10:47,48). And as Jesus enters the Holy City, David's Jerusalem, the crowds greet him in unmistakably messianic tones: "Blessed is the Kingdom of our Father David that is coming! Hosanna in the Highest" (11:10). Indeed Mark's description of the commanding presence of Jesus in the temple, teaching the crowds and overwhelming his opponents, brims with messianic tones (cf. 11-12).

A similar case could be made for the title "Son of God" in Mark. In Judaism this, too, was a title applied to the King. The installation of the King was described as God's beget-

---

[61] J. Donahue points out that in Judaism during the period current with the New Testament, heroic figures such as Solomon were portrayed as exorcists (cf. Donahue, "Temple, Trial, and Royal Christology," 73). On this see the discussion in G. Vermes, *Jesus the Jew* (New York: Macmillan, 1973), 58-82.

ting of him as "Son" (cf. Psalm 2:7;89:26-27). When Nathan
promised an enduring dynasty to David, he gave to David
God's promise of an offspring of whom it is said, "I will be
his father and he shall be my son" (II Sam 7:14). Therefore,
"Son of God" was used as a royal messianic title. Some
interpreters of Mark have argued that in his Gospel the title
has been heavily influenced by Hellenistic thought and
beyond the messianic significance derived from Judaism
connotes a divine being or "divine man" imbued with
ecstatic and miracle-working power as in some expressions
of ancient Greco-Roman tradition. But the existence of
such a "divine man" tradition contemporary with Mark's
Gospel is problematic.[62] It is more likely that Mark's community was strongly influenced by Jewish messianic tradition. However for Mark, as for the rest of the New
Testament, the Son of God title takes on additional nuance
because of its application to Jesus. His extraordinary relationship to God and his exaltation in resurrection add to the
title a sense of the ultimate authority and union with God
unique to Jesus.[63]

    The extraordinary circumstances in which this title is ap-
plied to Jesus in Mark bear out this rich complex of meaning
for the Son of God title. The Gospel begins with that designation: "The beginning of the Gospel of Jesus Christ, "Son
of God" (1:1).[64] But other uses are even more indicative.
Twice in the Gospel the title is used in theophanies where a
heavenly voice (=God) declares Jesus as "Son" — the baptism (1:11) and transfiguration (9:7). And in a scene that

---

[62] A popular exponent of "divine man" influence on Mark's christology has been
T. Weeden's work, *Mark: Traditions in Conflict* (Philadelphis: Fortress, 1971). A
more careful examination of this supposed tradition can be found in D. Tiede, *The
Charismatic Figure as Miracle Worker* (Society of Biblical Literature Dissertation
Series 1;Missoula: Scholars Press, 1972) and M. Hengel, *The Son of God* (Phila-
delphia: Fortress, 1976), 31-33.

[63] Cf. J. Dunn, *Christology in the Making* (Philadelphia: Westminster, 1980),
22-64.

[64] In some manuscript traditions "Son of God" is missing from Mark's opening
verse. However, the weight of evidence suggests that the title was originally part of
the verse.

also has a dramatic revelatory character, the centurion at the cross declares that Jesus was truly "Son of God" (15:39).[65]

Therefore both of the awesome titles cited in the High Priest's question — Christ and Son of God — have been applied to Jesus in Mark's Gospel. Jesus' response — "I am" — comes as no surprise to the reader. Hoever, Jesus' firm acceptance of the titles only under these circumstances, and his additional prediction about the coming "*Son of Man*" (14:62) reveal an important subtlety in Mark's use of titles for Jesus. Jesus' identity as Messiah and Son of God is apparent to the reader but seems hidden or at best misunderstood by most of the characters of the Gospel, especially outside of the passion story. Only God and the demons —supernatural beings — seem to recognize Jesus as Son of God. The scribes interpret Jesus' exorcisms not as messianic acts but as signs of collusion with Satan (3:22) and the Jewish leaders challenge his authority in the temple (11:27-33). His disciples too, as we have noted, seem unable to grasp Jesus' identity. Peter's confession of him as "the Christ" is accurate but his subsequent rebuke to Jesus puts the validity of that confession in doubt (8:27-33). Zebedee's sons ask to share in Jesus' power but their notion of it seems to be challenged by Jesus' own teaching (10:35-45). Jesus himself seems diffident about his messianic work: injunctions to silence and discretion follow many of the miracles (1:44; 5:43; 7:36; 8:26) and after the transfiguration (where he is declared Son) he explicitly cautions the three witnesses "to tell no one what they had seen, until the *Son of Man* had risen from the dead" (9:9).

---

[65] In two other instances demons recognize Jesus as "Son of God" (3:11) and "Son of the Most High God" (5:7; cf. the similar "Holy One of God" in 1:24). These are part of the struggle between Jesus and the demons. They attempt to exercise power over Jesus by naming him but he is able to silence them (cf. 1:25; 3:12). While this kind of struggle was a traditional element of exorcism stories, the naming of Jesus by the demons also allows Mark to confirm for the reader that supernatural beings recognize Jesus' true identity even though the human actors in the Gospel have failed to do so.

All of this intriguing material points to the fact that for Mark the cross is the touchstone for authentic confession of Jesus. Only in the passion story, when Jesus can be understood on the Gospel's own terms, are the royal messianic titles accepted by Jesus without qualification. This seems to be one of the major purposes of the Son of Man title, as we have already suggested.[66] It, too, is a title of exaltation, applied to the Risen Jesus who is exalted by God and will come in triumph at the end of the world to gather his chosen ones (13:26). In his acts of forgiveness (2:10) and his compassionate interpretation of the Sabbath laws (2:28), the earthly Jesus already exhibits the majestic power of the "Son of Man who is to come."

But for Mark, Jesus is revealed as Son of Man especially in his giving of life on behalf of the many (10:45). The very paradox of the Gospel rests here: where worldly standards can see only weakness, God's transforming power is present. In almost every instance in which Jesus speaks of his death he uses the Son of Man designation (cf. 8:31; 9:9,12,31; 10:33,45; 14:21,41). This title, in effect, adds the dimension of the cross to Christian understanding of Jesus' messianic authority. It, therefore, serves as a "corrective" or "completion" to other titles such as "Christ" or "Son of God." Not in the sense that Mark denies those traditional designations for Jesus but, through his Son of Man theology, the evangelist is able to give them their full Christian meaning.[67] Thus when Peter confesses Jesus as the "Christ" at Caesarea Philippi (8:29), Jesus charges him to silence (8:30) and begins to teach them that "the *Son of Man* must suffer many things..." (8:31). The whole "secrecy" motif in Mark has this net effect — Jesus' acts of power cannot be properly understood until their ultimate spirit and purpose are revealed in Jesus' use of power not to oppress but to give life to others (10:42-45). The act that reveals such use of power is the cross. Therefore, prior to the passion, Jesus' messianic

---

[66] Cf. above, pp. 28-30.

[67] For a full discussion of the relationship of the Son of Man title in 14:62 with the rest of Mark's Gospel, cf. N. Perrin, "The High Priest's Question and Jesus' Answer," in W. Kelber (ed.), *The Passion in Mark*, 81-93.

acts are shrouded in mystery and even Jesus seems to be diffident about their being widely broadcast (cf. 1:44; 5:43; 7:36). This background is in full play at the trial. In the context of the passion Jesus can reply unequivocally to the High Priest's question: "Are you the Christ, the Son of the Blessed?" (14:61). Jesus' "I am" (*ego eimi*) is a solemn affirmation of his messianic identity. In the final discourse, Jesus had warned his disciples about false Christs who would come claiming "I am" (*ego eimi*; cf. 13:6). Now, as a prisoner about to die, the true Messiah claims his title: "I am."

But here, too, the Son of Man designation is brought forward, this time not with explicit connection to Jesus' death — since the whole context provides that dimension — but as a prediction of triumph: "You will see the Son of Man sitting at the right hand of power, and coming with the clouds of heaven" (14:62). The solemn predictions on the journey from Galilee to Jerusalem spoke not only of the Son of Man's suffering but of his victory in resurrection. "After three days he will rise" (cf. 8:31; 9:31; 10:34; also 9:9). Here, too, in the midst of Jesus' passion, that promise of triumph is hurled at those who would destroy him. In this instance, as in 13:26, the triumph referred to is Jesus' exaltation at the right hand of God and his victorious return at the end of the age. The words used to describe this seem to be a composite of Old Testament citations. The apocalyptic vision in Daniel (7:13) spoke of a triumphant figure in human form ("one like a son of man") coming "*with the clouds of heaven.*" In Psalm 110 the king is addressed by God: "Sit at *my right hand*, till I make your enemies your footstool" (Ps 110:1). Both of these texts acclaim God's glorious power bestowed on the king (as in Ps. 110) or Israel (probably in Daniel 7:13). Christian reflection even prior to Mark may have blended these Old Testament texts and applied them to Jesus' triumph at the end of the world.[68]

---

[68] This thesis has been strongly advocated by N. Perrin. He conceives of this process as a Christian *pesher*, similar to the interpretation process at Qumran, in which Old Testament texts were blended and adapted to express the community's theological perspective. Cf. further, N. Perrin, *A Modern Pilgrimage in New Testament Christology*, 11-40.

In the context of 14:62 this response of Jesus is a challenge
to his opponents and, for the Christian reader of the Gospel,
a glorious promise of hope: "*you* will see...." In the discourse on the Mount of Olives, Jesus had promised that
after the travails of persecution and world chaos, the world
would *see* the Son of Man come to gather a community
from the four winds and from the corners of the earth
(13:26-27). The Gospel would end with a similar promise:
the women who come to the empty tomb are sent to the
broken and scattered disciples with a message of hope:
"...he is going before you to Galilee, there you will *see* him,
as he told you" (16:7). To "see" Jesus meant not only to
encounter the Risen Christ, but to take up the mission
begun in Galilee and to preach the Gospel to the whole
world, awaiting that final "seeing" when the triumphant
Jesus would return to gather his people.[69] Therefore the
phrase, "you will see" in 14:62 is a challenge to Jesus'
enemies and a comfort for his church.

The reader of the Gospel knows that Jesus' promise of
triumph will be fulfilled but the full agony of the passion is
yet to be experienced. The High Priest dramatically rejects
Jesus' claim to authority by tearing his garments and label-
ing Jesus' declaration as "blasphemy" (14:63-64). The rending of one's garments was the proper reaction to blasphemy,
as when King Hezekiah and his ministers tore their garments in reaction to an Assyrian official's blasphemous
challenge to the power of the God of Israel (II Kings 18:
37-19:4).

It is not clear why Jesus' answer is termed "blasphemy."
Historically, blasphemy referred to the sacrilegious uttering
of the divine name. But it is hard to see how the High Priest
could have construed Jesus' reply as this type of sacrilege.
Jesus even speaks indirectly of "*Power*" rather than the right
hand of "*God*."[70] Whatever may have been the historical
realities, in Mark's account Jesus' claim to messianic
authority and ultimate triumph is rejected in the strongest

---

[69] Cf. below, Part III, pp. 151-153.

[70] The charge of blasphemy is referred to in Leviticus 24:10-16. On this point, cf.
further, J. Blinzler, *The Trial of Jesus*, 153-54, D. Catchpole, *The Trial of Jesus*,
195-96.

possible way. No more witnesses are needed; Jesus' declaration is sufficient for judgment. The High Priest puts the decisive question to the Sanhedrin: "What is your decision?" Their judgment is without hesitation: "And they all condemned him as deserving death" (14:64). The irony of the passion story continues to run deep. For the Sanhedrin, as characters within the drama, Jesus' death would appear to be the end of his messianic pretensions. But the Christian reader knows that precisely through the death they impose Jesus' messianic power will be complete.

The trial scene ends with mockery (just as the Roman trial will, cf. 15:16-20). "Some" (apparently members of the Sanhedrin), begin to spit at him and "cover his face" and to strike him. The guards join in the blows (14:65). This abject scene of torture and derision jolts the reader back into the reality of suffering. But at the same time Mark reaffirms the Gospel's conviction about Jesus' identity and the ultimate efficacy of his pain. Description of the torment rained on Jesus echoes Isaiah's portrayal of the Suffering Servant who atones for the sins of Israel:

> "I gave my back to the smiters,
> and my cheeks to those who pulled
> out the beard;
> I hid not my face from shame
> and spitting. (Is 50:6)

The entire scene — Jesus surrounded by tormentors — recalls the assault on the servant and on the Just One of Israel.

The taunt "Prophesy!" (14:65) is a final ironic commentary on the scene. Jesus' prophetic words of judgment over the temple and his claims concerning the Son of Man's coming triumph are mocked. So, too, are Jesus' messianic claims which are a major issue of this scene (cf. 14:61-62). All of this is rejected and hurled back at the victim who is the target of his enemies' blows: "Prophesy!" The Christian reader is reminded again that Jesus' power is not exercised according to the world's pattern.

C) PETER'S DENIAL (14:66-72)

The floodlights of Mark's drama shift once again as the reader's attention is turned from Jesus surrounded by tormentors to Peter, the last of the disciples, warming himself before the fire in the courtyard below the trial chamber (14:66-67; cf. 14:53-54). The scene that now unfolds is poignant and expertly constructed. Peter's apostasy flares up like a smoldering fire bursting into flame. The accusations begin as a private confrontation between Peter and a servant girl (14:66-67) but quickly mushroom to repeated accusations in earshot of bystanders (14:69), and finally spread to the bystanders themselves (14:70). Peter's denials, similarly, begin as feigned ignorance of what the maid says (14:68,70) but burst into panicked cursing and an oath denying his relationship to Jesus (14:71). Meanwhile Peter retreats, moving from his position in the courtyard (14:66) out to the gate (14:68). Over the entire scene hangs Jesus' words of prophecy. The haunting signal of the cockcrow (14:72) triggers Peter's bitter tears of failure and remorse as he remembers Jesus' warning at the passover meal (14:30).

Peter's denial of Jesus was most probably a historical fact. It is unlikely that the early community would create such an astounding story for mere effect, nor is there any real evidence of an anti-Petrine movement in early Christianity, as some have alleged.[71] But for Mark this story serves as a crucial reflection on discipleship. The fact that the Peter story frames Jesus' confession before the Sanhedrin shows Mark's hand; Jesus' fearless confession is in bold contrast to Peter's frightened denial. The dialogue in the scene also shows the evangelist's absorption with discipleship. On the one hand, the accusations against Peter ironically stress his bonds with Jesus: "You were *with* the Nazarene, *Jesus*" (v.67); "this man is *one of them*" (v.69); "certainly you are *one of them*; for you are a *Galilean*"

---

[71] See, for example, the conjectures of K. Dewey, "Peter's Curse and Cursed Peter in W. Kelber (ed.), (Mark 14:53-54, 66-72)," *The Passion in Mark*, 106-14. On Petrine traditions in the New Testament, cf. R. Brown, et. al, *Peter In the New Testament* (New York: Paulist, 1973).

(v.70). The charge of being a "Galilean" refers, on the surface, to the district's dialect that Peter presumably speaks. But for the reader of the Gospel a deeper meaning is unavoidable. Galilee had been the place of Jesus' Kingdom ministry (1:14-15), the place where Peter had received the gift of discipleship (1:16-20), and where Jesus had already promised to meet his disciples in reconciliation after his resurrection (14:28; 16:7).

Similarly the wording of Peter's denials also recall Mark's discipleship motifs.[72] He claims to "neither know nor understand" the maid's words (14:68) and in his final denial, swears "I do not know the man of whom you speak" (14:71). Metaphors of "knowing" and "understanding" are an essential part of the language Mark uses for faith in Jesus. The parables, as veiled speech, are baffling to those who reject Jesus so that they "may see but not perceive, and may indeed hear but not understand..." (4:12). Even though the disciples have been destined to receive the secret of the Kingdom (4:11), they themselves do not "understand" (4:13, *oidate*, the same Greek word for "knowing" or "understanding" used in 14:71). The disciples' failure to recognize Jesus in his walking on the sea is characterized as lack of understanding and hardness of heart (6:52). In another sea story their repeated failure to understand Jesus' warnings about the leaven of the Pharisees and Herod brings a strong indictment, all of it couched in perception metaphors drawn from the same text of Isaiah 6:6-8 quoted in the parable discourse (4:12):

> "Do you not perceive or understand? Are your hearts hardened? Having eyes do you not see, and having ears do you not hear? And do you not remember?... Do you not yet understand?" (8:17-18,21)

A failure to understand characterizes the reactions of the disciples to Jesus' passion predictions in 9:32, as it does

[72] On Mark's portrayal of the disciples and pertinent literature on this theme, cf. above, Part I, pp. 31-35.

Peter's bafflement at the transfiguration (9:6). Thus the reader is not surprised to hear Peter's denial couched in similar terms. As the false witnesses at the trial and the mockers who taunted Jesus, Peter speaks an ironic truth: "I do not *know* this man of whom you speak" (14:71). The reader who witnessed Peter's attempt to "muzzle" Jesus at the first teaching on the passion (8:32, the word *epitiman* used here implies a violent silencing) and his false bravado at the Passover meal (14:29,31) could only conclude that the leader indeed did not yet comprehend Jesus as the Son of Man destined for the cross.

The story concludes with Peter's collapse (*epibalōn*) in tears (14:72). Mark does not elaborate but in view of the promise of discipleship renewal made by Jesus at the supper (14:28), the reader can surmise that these are not tears of despair but of remorse which will ultimately lead to repentance. When the young man at the tomb gives the women their charge to bring Jesus' resurrection message to the disciples, it is phrased "tell the disciples *and Peter*" (16:7), the same sequence in which their discipleship had failed.

The promise of reconciliation and eventual discipleship renewal may give us a key to another function of the startling failures in the passion story. Mark's story portrays the inner circle of Jesus' community fleeing in fear, with the leader denying his master with curses and perjury. Yet, despite such scandalous failure they are forgiven by Jesus and restored to their mission.

One can surmise the impact of such stories on Mark's community if, as seems to be the case, it had been buffeted by persecution. The Gospel's focus on the passion, as well as its explicit references to persecution (4:17; 10:30,39; 13:9,11-13), are good reasons to believe that Mark's community had already experienced the cost of discipleship, probably under the persecution of Nero at Rome. Such persecution produced courageous martyrs but also led to apostasy and desertion as many Christians sagged under the torment and pressures brought to bear on the community. The allegorization of the seed parable speaks in exactly these terms when explaining the seed sown on rocky soil: "And these in like manner are the ones sown upon rocky ground, who, when they hear the word, immediately receive it with joy; and they have no root in themselves, but endure for a while; then, *when tribulation or persecution arises on account of the word*, immediately they fall away" (4:16-17).

If such failures had been experienced by Mark's church then one can also guess that after the heat of persecution had abated, the issue of reconciliation with those who had abandoned the community but now were drifting back would be painful. Recrimination and hatred between "resistance" and "collaborators" in the aftermath of persecution or oppression is often more brutal and divisive than the persecution itself. Mark's stories would have a potent effect on a community context such as this.[73] Could reconciliation be denied to fallen disciples when such a passion story was proclaimed? Along with the example of courage and fidelity provided by the woman who anointed Jesus (cf. above 14:3-9) the flight of the disciples and the denial of Peter would, paradoxically, become "gospel," that is, good news for a Christian community that knew "failures" as well as heroes.

V. The Trial Before Pilate: Jesus the King (15:1-20a)

The coming of dawn and the transfer of location from the house of the High Priest to the court of Pilate signal another major change of scene in Mark's passion story. After the transfer to Pilate (15:1) the narrative is composed of three brief episodes: an initial interrogation of Jesus by Pilate (15:2-5), the choice between Jesus and Barabbas (15:6-15), and the mockery of Jesus (15:16-20a). In each scene the issue of Jesus' royal messianic identity is central.

---

73. This would be especially true if, as would seem to be the case, the church Mark addressed was composed of many small groupings or "house churches." Divisions within such a small arena would make confrontation and conflict much more intense.

¹And as soon as it was morning the chief priests, with the elders and scribes, and the whole council held a consultation; and they bound Jesus and led him away and delivered him to Pilate. ²And Pilate asked him, "Are you the King of the Jews?" And he answered him, "You have said so." ³And the chief priests accused him of many things. ⁴And Pilate again asked him, "Have you no answer to make? See how many charges they bring against you." ⁵But Jesus made no further answer, so that Pilate wondered.

⁶Now at the feast he used to release for them one prisoner for whom they asked. ⁷And among the rebels in prison, who had committed murder in the insurrection, there was a man called Barabbas. ⁸And the crowd came up and began to ask Pilate to do as he was wont to do for them. ⁹And he answered them, "Do you want me to release for you the King of the Jews?"¹⁰For he perceived that it was out of envy that the chief priests had delivered him up." ¹¹But the chief priests stirred up the crowd to have him release for them Barabbas instead. ¹²And Pilate again said to them, "Then what shall I do with the man whom you call the King of the Jews?" ¹³And they cried out again, "Crucify him." ¹⁴And Pilate said to them, "Why, what evil has he done?" But they shouted all the more, "Crucify him." ¹⁵So Pilate, wishing to satisfy the crowd, released for them Barabbas; and having scourged Jesus, he delivered him to be crucified.

¹⁶And the soldiers led him away inside the palace (that is, the praetorium); and they called together the whole battalion. ¹⁷And they clothed him in a purple cloak, and plaiting a crown of thorns they put it on him. ¹⁸And they began to salute him, "Hail, King of the Jews!" ¹⁹And they struck his head with a reed, and spat upon him, and they knelt down in homage to him. ²⁰And when they had mocked him, they stripped him of the purple cloak, and put his own clothes on him. And they led him out to crucify him. (15:1-20a)

A) THE INTERROGATION: "ARE YOU THE KING OF THE JEWS?" (15:1-5)

The pace of events quickens noticeably as Mark turns from the trial before the Sanhedrin to the climactic scene with the Romans. The opening verse of chapter 15 provides that transition. The events and decisions of the preceding night are summed up as the whole Sanhedrin gathers at dawn. In Mark's account the formal decision had been taken the night before (14:64). This meeting at dawn seems to be merely a strategy session or consultation prior to approaching Pilate. The gathering also enables Mark to reassert the agency of the Jewish leaders as the primary opponents of Jesus.[74] It is *they* who "bind" Jesus, "lead him away" and "hand him over" to Pilate. The verb used to describe the latter action is *paradidomi*, which has been used with quasi-technical force in reference to Jesus' deliverance to death.[75] Judas had "handed over" Jesus to the leaders (14:10-11,18,21,41,42,44 — the word *paradidomi* is used in each instance); and they would be the agents as Jesus is "handed over" for the final time to the Gentiles. The third and most detailed of the passion predictions had described this exact sequence: "the Son of Man will be *delivered (paradothēsetai)* to the chief priests and the scribes, and they will condemn him to death, and *deliver (paradōsousin) him to the Gentiles. . ." (10:32).*

Pilate is mentioned without introduction (15:1). Apparently his role was well known to Mark's readers. He was the fifth Roman procurator of Judea and held office from A.D.26-36. Both Josephus and Philo, Jewish historians contemporary with this period, speak of Pilate as cruel and arbitrary. The general portrayal of him in the Gospels is less

---

74 On this point, cf. above, pp. 20-29. Note that Matthew has a different version of events at this point. Unlike Mark's account, no decision is reached during the night "trial" (compare Mk 14:64 and Mt 26:66 where the Sanhedrin says Jesus "deserves" death but does not "judge" him as in Mark). That decision only comes in the morning: cf. Mt 27:1.

75 Cf. above, p. 17, n.4.

negative; he seems unconvinced of Jesus' guilt and gives in reluctantly to the demands of the Jewish leaders and the pressure of the crowds. It is clearly the role of the Jewish leaders which is more decisive for the Gospel writers. This may stem from apologetic motifs, downplaying the role of the Romans and stressing Jesus' innocence (even in the eyes of the Roman governor) in order to assure Roman authorities that Christianity was not inherently seditious. But the motives are also theological. The Gospel concentrates more on the role of the Sanhedrin because Jesus' rejection by Israel had far greater religious implications than his condemnation by Pilate.

The messianic identity of Jesus had been the major motif of the trial before the Sanhedrin. Jesus was indeed the Christ, the Son of the Blessed, but he was also the suffering and ultimately triumphant Son of Man. The true nature of Jesus' role as Messiah could only be understood in the light of the Cross. The same paradox will be at work in the trial before Pilate.[76] All of the foes who circle around Jesus deny him the title of King. The Sanhedrin seeks to have him condemned by the Romans for pretending to political power. The procurator refuses to accept their accusations and only in mockery applies the title to Jesus. The crowds choose Barabbas and reject Jesus as their King. And, finally, the Roman soldiers torment Jesus, forcing upon him a royal parody. But for the reader the irony of the passion story is again in play: Jesus *is* a King, but, as the taunts and mockeries of Jesus' opponents unwittingly affirm, *not* a king in the human mode of power.

Mark's account of the interrogation is lean (15:3-5). No physical setting is given at all. Only in 15:16 do we learn that the trial probably took place outside the "praetorium" when the soldiers lead him inside for the mockery. The reader must supply the transition as Pilate's initial question plunges into the key issue: "Are you the King of the Jews?"

---

[76] Mark's emphasis on the royal messianic identity of Jesus in the Roman trial scene is a major focus of F. Matera, *The Kingship of Jesus: Composition and Theology in Mark 15* (SBL Dissertation Series 66; Chico, CA: Scholars Press, 1982).

(15:2). The title "King of the *Jews*" is applied to Jesus only in the Roman trial and apparently has a more political cast to it. The title "King of *Israel*" would have a more religious connotation (cf. 15:32 where it is placed on the lips of the chief priests and scribes in apposition to "Christ"); whereas the Romans, fearing political sedition, would use the more secular term "King of the *Jews*." Only as the scene unfolds do we have confirmed what the reader can only infer at this point: the Jewish leaders have accused Jesus of pretending to be a king (15:12 "the man *you call* the King of the Jews"; also 15:9-10).

Jesus' response — "you say so" (15:2) — is ambiguous. It is surely less affirmative than the resounding "I am" that greeted the High Priest's question in 14:62. But neither is it negative. In Matthew's passion when Judas asks Jesus if he were the betrayer, Jesus' reply is similar: "You have said so" (*su eipas*, 26:25). In this instance the reply of Jesus is surely an affirmative one, but the phrase shifts the emphasis to the fact that Judas himself has made the statement: "*you* have said so." The phrase in Mark may have a similar function. *Pilate* has said it: Jesus is "King of the Jews." Because of the formulation of the title and Pilate's incredulity, Jesus' answer is less than a resounding affirmative. Yet because the political title points to a fundamental truth about Jesus' identity, neither is it denied.

The remainder of the trial recalls the scene before the Sanhedrin. The leaders accuse him of many things, leading Pilate to probe Jesus for a response in words almost identical to those of the High Priest at the Jewish hearing: "Have you no answer to make? See how many charges they bring against you" (15:4).[77] Now, as before, Jesus' response to the avalanche of false testimony is silence (compare 15:5 and 14:61). That silence will hold until the piercing lament at the moment of Jesus' death (15:34). Once again the passion story evokes the memory both of the Just One, surrounded

---

[77] Compare with 14:60, "*Have you no answer to make?* What is it that these men testify *against you?*"

by accusers and abandoned by friends, and of God's silent Servant (Is 53:7). Even Pilate's amazement at Jesus' silence seems to echo the impact of the Suffering Servant:

> [14] As many were astonished at him—
> his appearance was so marred, beyond
> human semblance,
> and his form beyond that of the sons of men—
> [15] so shall he startle many nations;
> kings shall shut their mouths because of him...
>   (Is 52:14-15)

Nor could the attentive reader of Mark forget the warnings of the final discourse: "But take heed to yourselves; for they will deliver you up to councils; . . . and you will stand before governors and kings for my sake, to bear testimony before them" (13:9). . . "and when they bring you to trial and deliver you up, do not be anxious beforehand what you are to say; but say whatever is given you in that hour, for it is not you who speak, but the Holy Spirit" (13:11). Mark presents Jesus as the first in a long line of those who would suffer unjust accusations and be brought to trial for the sake of the gospel.[78]

B) JESUS OR BARABBAS? (15:6-14)

The Barabbas episode advances Mark's purpose in this part of the passion story. Pilate's conviction that Jesus is innocent and the leaders' blind intent to destroy Jesus become even more apparent. But so, too, does the nature of Jesus' royal identity.

There is no historical information about the custom of releasing a prisoner on the Passover other than what is found in the four Gospels. It is unlikely, however, that such an unusual event would have been fabricated by the tradition. Release of a prisoner fits into the liberation motif of the Jewish Passover and may have been a concession on the part of the Roman administration of Judea.[79]

[78] Cf. above, Part I, pp. 37-39.

[79] See the discussion in R. Pesch, *Das Markusevangelium* II, 462.

Mark tersely briefs the reader on the custom (15:6) and the fact that Barabbas, who would become the crowd's candidate for release, was a rebel and a murderer (15:7). We are also told that the choice rests with the *crowd* (15:6,8) thereby introducing a new element into the dynamics of the passion. Until this point Jesus has been confronted by the hostile Jewish leaders, the armed band sent to arrest him (14:43, also called a "crowd" but presumably not the same as the crowd in 15:8), and Judas, the betrayer. Now the crowds who had been generally neutral and sometimes even approving of Jesus (cf. 11:18; 12:12,37) would be turned against him by his opponents (15:11). The Marcan Jesus is being stripped of every support.

The crowd surges forward, now in direct dialogue with Pilate (15:8). Mark deftly presents the scene as a cold choice between Barabbas, a rebel and murderer, and Jesus, the "King of the Jews." Pilate's question trumpets the underlying issue: "Do you want me to release for you the King of the Jews?" (15:9). But the crowd, swayed by the chief priests, demands Barabbas (15:11). Pilate, in turn, tests the crowd by suggesting Jesus because, as Mark notes, the chief priests had delivered Jesus out of "envy" (15:10). The word used here for "envy" (*phthonos*) has connotations of malicious intent or spite. The Book of Wisdom assigns "envy" (*phthonos*) as the devil's motivation for bringing death into the world (Wis 2:24).

The sequence of Pilate's question and the crowd's response is repeated again, but this time the drama mounts to its awesome climax (15:12-14). Pilate's question puts Jesus' fate in the hands of the crowd. Instead of asking, "Whom do you want me to release for you?" the question becomes "What shall I do with the man whom you call the King of the Jews?" (15:12). The crowd now utters the words towards which the entire passion story has been targeted: "crucify him" (15:13). Pilate's protest about Jesus' innocence is only met with increased determination on the part of the crowd: "crucify him!" (15:14).

Only now, when the crowd's rejection of Jesus and the choice of Barabbas have been rigidly determined does

Pilate's formal decision come. Right to the end the Roman procurator's initiative is minimized: "wishing to satisfy the crowd" (15:15). Barabbas is released and given to the crowd, while Jesus is scourged and "handed over" to be crucified. Scourging of a prisoner prior to execution on the cross was widespread Roman custom. Once again the word "handed over" (*paredōkon*) is used, now to describe a final transfer, from Pilate to the executioners.

The Barabbas story drives the wedge more deeply between the Gospel's notion of power and that of the "world," with the device of irony again playing its decisive role. The crowds, now sharing in the blindness of the Sanhedrin, refuse to accept Jesus as "King of the Jews." Instead they choose for themselves a man labeled as a rebel and a murderer. Pilate, a Roman ruler, speaks in favor of Jesus while Jesus' own people condemn him to crucifixion. Only the reader of Mark's text is in a position to see through the merging ironies of the scene. Jesus, the Christ, the Son of God, is, indeed, the King of the Jews. The crowds along with the Sanhedrin join a sad cast of characters in the Gospel who find Jesus an "obstacle" and cannot recognize his messianic identity. The Barabbas incident adds another dimension. Jesus' power is not to be found with "swords and clubs," as he had challenged the mob in Gethsemane (14:47-49). The way of the Son of Man is the cross.

C) MOCKERY OF THE KING (15:16-20)

The last episode connected with the trial brings the motif of Jesus' messianic identity to its most forceful expression. Jesus is led into the praetorium where the entire battalion of Roman soldiers gathers to mock his alleged claims to kingship.

This mockery, too, had been predicted by Jesus (cf. 10:33, "and they will mock him and spit upon him") and its execution is described in detail. The soldiers enrobe Jesus in mock royal garments, a "purple cloak" (the traditional color for royalty) and a "crown of thorns" (15:17). Once Jesus is dressed for the role, the parody escalates into cruel violence.

The soldiers salute him with, "Hail, King of the Jews," directly taking up the chief accusation at the trial, just as the mockery of the Sanhedrin had taken up the theme of the Jewish trial (cf. above 14:65). He is struck on the head with a reed, the royal head that an anonymous disciple had lavishly anointed at the beginning of the passion (14:3). He is spat upon (as in the previous mockery, 14:65) and, finally, offered taunting homage (15:19). When the vicious game is spent, the soldiers strip off his "royal" garments and prepare him for execution (15:20).

Such abuse of a prisoner by a band of soldiers has infinite analogies in the history of humanity. The Christians of Mark's day may have experienced similar brutalizations in the cause of the Gospel. Several accounts from the ancient world bear similarity to the scene in Mark and there is no reason to doubt that such abuse was in fact heaped on Jesus, a Jewish prisoner, condemned for royal pretensions and in the hands of soldiers whose own duties would hardly make them sympathetic to such a criminal.

But the function of the story in Mark's narrative is not simply to report the abuse suffered by Jesus nor to offer an example of martyrdom. The vivid parody of the trappings of worldly kings intensifies the irony that suffuses this whole section of Mark's narrative. From the reader's privileged perspective, the soldiers continue their blind rejection of Jesus. They mock one who is, in fact, a king. But the irony shifts in another direction, too. The unlikely trappings of kingship on a flogged and condemned prisoner expose the truth: Jesus' authority and power as the Christ will not be exercised in the lordly ways of human power. The all important dialogue of Jesus with the disciples outside of Jericho is vividly illustrated here:

> "You know that those who are supposed to rule over the Gentiles lord it over them, and their great ones exercise power over them. But it shall not be so among you; but whoever would be great among you must be your servant, and whoever would be first among you must be the slave of all. For the Son of Man also came not to be served but

to serve, and to give his life as a ransom for many"
(10:44-45).

Mark's insistence on the cross as the consummate expression both of Jesus' mission and of authentic discipleship is absolutely consistent.

VI. Crucifixion and Death (Mark 15:20b-41)

Departure from the praetorium for Golgotha signals the climax of Mark's drama. Three scenes, each marked by the passage of time, bring Jesus to crucifixion (15:20b-24), final mockery (15:25-32) and death (15:33-41).

[20]And they led him out to crucify him. [21]And they compelled a passer-by, Simon of Cyrene, who was coming in from the country, the father of Alexander and Rufus, to carry his cross. [22]And they brought him to the place called Golgotha (which means the place of a skull). [23]And they offered him wine mingled with myrrh; but he did not take it. [24]And they crucified him, and divided his garments among them, casting lots for them, to decide what each should take. [25]And it was the third hour, when they crucified him. [26]And the inscription of the charge against him read, "The King of the Jews." [27]And with him they crucified two robbers, one on his right and one on his left. [29]And those who passed by derided him, wagging their heads, and saying, "Aha!" You who would destroy the temple and build it in three days, [30]save yourself, and come down from the cross!" [31]So also the chief priests mocked him to one another with the scribes, saying, "He saved others; he cannot save himself. [32]Let the Christ, the King of Israel, come down now from the cross, that we may see and believe." Those who were crucified with him also reviled him.

[33]And when the sixth hour had come, there was darkness over the whole land until the ninth hour. [34]And at the ninth hour Jesus cried with a loud voice, "*Eloi, Eloi, lama sabachthani?*" which means, "My God, my God, why has thou forsaken me?" [35]And some of the bystanders hearing it said, "Behold, he is calling Elijah." [36]And one ran and, filling a sponge full of vinegar, put it on a reed and gave it to him to drink, saying, "Wait, let us see whether Elijah will come to take him down." [37]And Jesus uttered a loud cry, and breathed his last. [38]And the curtain of the temple was torn in two, from top to bottom. [39]And when the centurion, who stood facing him, saw that he thus breathed his last, he said, "Truly this man was the Son of God!" [40]There were also women looking on from afar, among whom were Mary Magdalene, and Mary the mother of James the younger and of Joses, and Salome, [41]who, when he was in Galilee, followed him, and ministered to him; and also many other women who came up with him to Jerusalem. (15:20b-41)

A) GOLGOTHA (15:20b-24)

Mark's account of the crucifixion of Jesus is stark and unembroidered, reflecting the noteworthy restraint of the passion tradition in its description of the physical torments of Jesus. The details given harmonize with what we know of crucifixion procedures in this period.[80]

As Jesus is led out from the praetorium to the place of execution, the soldiers impound a passer-by, Simon of Cyrene, to carry Jesus' cross (15:2). Prisoners condemned to crucifixion were made to carry their own cross, or at least the crossbeam. This may suggest that Jesus was already severely weakened by the flogging and torture he had

---

[80] Cf. M. Hengel, *Crucifixion* (Philadelphia: Fortress, 1977) and J. Fitzmyer, "Crucifixion in Palestine, Qumran, and the New Testament," *The Catholic Biblical Quarterly* 40 (1978), 493-513.

endured (15:5-20). Simon, we are told, was the "father of Alexander and Rufus." These names seem to be known to the Marcan community or at least to the tradition the evangelist incorporates at this point (note that Matthew and Luke drop this detail, cf. Mt 27:32; Lk 23:26). Simon must have been a diaspora Jew (Cyrene is in northern Africa) who had come to the city for the pilgrimage feast of Passover. The names of his sons are common Greek (not Jewish) names.[81] He is apparently returning to the city "from the fields." Mark does not explicitly say Simon was working in the fields so it is useless to speculate how this detail might conflict with the Jewish law's prohibition against working on the feastday.

Despite the terseness of the narration, there is some indication that Mark suggests a symbolic role for Simon. He "takes up his (Jesus') cross"; these are the exact words used in 8:34, "If any one would come after me, let him deny himself and *take up his cross* and follow me." Simon, who moves through the passion story without introduction or epilogue, reminds the reader of the cost of discipleship.[82]

Jesus is brought to the place of execution, which according to both Jewish and Roman law was to be outside of the city. Mark informs us that the place was called "Golgotha," an Aramaic word which the evangelist promptly translates for his Greek-speaking readers as "skull place."[83] The name may have originally referred to the shape of the rock outcropping on which public executions were performed. Again in accordance with standard procedures, Jesus was offered a mild narcotic, wine mixed with myrrh, which he refused. Although Jesus' decision gives a sense of deliberate-

[81] A "Rufus" is mentioned in Romans 16:13, "Greet Rufus, eminent in the Lord, also his mother and mine..." But we cannot be sure this is the same man referred to by Mark. Both Alexander and Rufus were common names.

[82] Cf. W. Harrington, *Mark* (New Testament Message 4; Wilmington: Michael Glazier, Inc., 1979), 236.

[83] Mark makes similar explanatory translations in 5:41 (*Talitha cumi* translated as "Little girl, I say to you, arise"), 14:36 (*Abba* translated as "Father"), and 15:34 (where Jesus' final words, *Eloi, Eloi lama sabachthani* are translated as "My God, my God, why hast thou forsaken me?").

ness in this critical moment, Mark does not seem to linger over this detail. Matthew's version, by changing the word "myrrh" to vinegar or "gall" (*cholēs* Mt 27:34), aligns the incident with Psalm 69:21. "They gave me poison for food, and for my thirst they gave me vinegar,(*cholēs*) to drink," thereby making the offered drink another in a series of sufferings inflicted on the Just One of Israel. The actual moment of crucifixion is eloquently understated: "And they crucified him" (15:24). There are no details, no lingering over the physical horrors of this moment as Jesus, the Christ, the Son of God, is pinned to his instrument of death. Mark adds a note about the division of his garments; for the first time in this episode we have a clear allusion to the Scriptures. Psalm 22, a major expression of the suffering Just One motif, includes the division of garments as one of the desolating torments of God's faithful one: "They divide my garments among them and for my raiments they cast lots" (Ps 22:18). Mark will more fully exploit this psalm at the moment of Jesus' death (cf. 15:34).

B) FINAL MOCKERY (15:25-32)

The terse understatement of the crucifixion scene gives way to a cascade of abuse as Jesus is mounted on the cross before his enemies. It is one of Mark's most skillful narratives, catching up the major motifs of christology and discipleship that have run throughout the Gospel and bringing them to their final expression.

The third hour is noted (15:25), not only indicating a new phase of the drama but quickening the tension as the hour of death, the ninth (15:34), swiftly approaches. This time indication, the third hour, is retrospective, recalling the moment of crucifixion (15:24) yet also shifting the reader's attention forward, momentarily away from Jesus to the reaction of the onlookers.

The placard over the cross cites Jesus' "crime," allowing the ironic strains of the trial scenes to come back into play. The reader is fully aware that Jesus is the Christ, "The King of the Jews" (15:26). From the vantage point of Mark's theology that title has at last found its authentic place of proclamation — fastened on the cross of Jesus.

And two thieves or insurrectionists (the Greek term *lēstai* could mean either) are crucified with Jesus, "one on his right and one on his left" (15:27). This gruesome entourage continues the mockery of Jesus' kingship inflicted by the soldiers (15:16-20). Jesus the King is surrounded by a court of executed criminals, probably rebels, perhaps some of those arrested in the same insurrection with Barabbas (15:7). But ironic truth may be breaking through again in Mark's story. To be crucified with Jesus was, in fact, the promised lot of those who would be his followers (8:34-35) and when Zebedee's sons asked for places of power "one at your right hand and one at your left" (10:37) they had, instead, been promised a share in his passion (10:39).[84]

The ironic proclamation of Jesus as king draws a parade of mockers whose taunts review the major issues of the trial and indeed of the Gospel itself. The first, the passers-by (15:29), "blaspheme him" and "wag their heads," a taunting gesture drawn from Psalm 22:7: "All who see me mock at me, they make mouths at me, they wag their heads." No biblical piece more eloquently expresses the lament of the Just One of Israel than this Psalm and it is close to the surface in the entire crucifixion scene.[85] The assaults of the mockers demonstrate Jesus' unrelieved isolation in Mark's

[84] In the Greek text there is verbal identity between Jesus' replay of James and John's request ("but to sit *at my right hand* or *at my left* is not mine to grant...," 10:40) and the phrasing in 15:27. In some manuscript traditions an additional verse follows on 15:27 — "And the scripture was fulfilled which says, 'He was reckoned with the transgressors' " — an allusion to the Suffering Servant in Isaiah 53:12. However, evidence for this reading is not persuasive.

[85] On Psalm 22 and its role in the passion tradition, cf. L. R. Fischer, "Betrayed by Friends, An Expository Study of Psalm 22," *Interpretation* 18 (1964), 20-27; A. Feuillet, "Souffrance et confiance en Dieu. Commentaire du ps. 22," *Nouvelle Revue Theologique* 70 (1948), 137-49; H. Gese, "Psalm 22 und das Neue Testament. Der alteste Bericht vom Tode Jesus und die Entstehung des Herrenmahles," *Zeitschrift für Theologie und Kirche* 65 (1968), 1-22; H. D. Lange, "The Relationship Between Psalm 22 and the Passion Narrative," *Concordia Theological Monthly* 43 (1972), 610-21; J. Reumann, "Psalm 22 at the Cross," *Interpretation* 28 (1974), 39-58; H. J. Steichele, *Der leidende Sohn Gottes* (Regensburg: Frederich Pustet, 1980), 193-279. F. Matera, *The Kingship of Jesus*, 127-135.

presentation. Unlike Luke's account, no disciples remain, no crowd on the brink of repentance. Only when death has engulfed Jesus will the moment of vindication come.

The bystanders mock Jesus for his alleged threats against the temple: "Aha! You who would destroy the temple and build it in three days, save yourself, and come down from the cross" (15:29-30). The derisive words, "Aha!" again bring echoes of the lament psalms. ("they open wide their mouths against me; they say, 'Aha, Aha! our eyes have seen it...'" Psalm 35:21; also 40:15; 70:4). The reference to the destruction of the temple recalls, of course, the accusation brought against Jesus in the trial before the Sanhedrin (14:58). Jesus' claim to messianic authority is again rejected by his opponents.

The taunt, "save yourself and come down from the cross," reaches deeper into the heart of Mark's Gospel. There is a readily apparent surface logic to the mockers' words: one who claimed to have such power over the temple of God should be able to save his own life. But underneath the surface logic is a profound misconception of Jesus and his message encountered before in Mark's story. When Peter heard Jesus' first passion prediction he had attempted to stifle him (8:32); reference to the cross was rejected by the disciple. Jesus' own response was to gather the disciples and to instruct them that "whoever would save (*sōsai*) his life will lose it; and whoever loses his life for my sake and the gospel's will save it" (8:35). This kind of "logic" — take up the cross, and lose life to save it — directly contradicts the "wisdom" of the mockers: "save (*sōson*) yourself and come down from the cross." The attempt to separate Jesus from his cross through a different perception of his authority and mission is an alien spirit against which the entire Gospel of Mark is mobilized.

The chief priests and scribes come next in the parade of derision (15:31-32). Their taunts echo the sentiments of the bystanders and push the challenge to the gospel to its most intense expression. Their first remark is similar to the logic of the previous mockery, but shifts from Jesus' threat against the temple to his power to save: "He saved others he cannot save himself." The verb "save" (*sōzein*) used here is connected with healing in the Gospel, expressing the liberating transformation effected by Jesus' power. The woman with the hemorrhage (5:23, 28), the sick in the villages around Gennesaret (6:56), and blind Bartimaeus (10:52) are all "saved" by Jesus. In the conflict story over a Sabbath cure, Jesus had challenged his opponents' interpretation of law and, at the same time, exposed his own commitment: "Is it lawful on the Sabbath to do good or to do harm, to save (*sōzein*) life or to kill?" (3:4). These salvation experiences are only a few of the many other outpourings of compassionate strength in the Gospel where, even though the word is not used, Jesus "saves" broken humanity. Thus the mockers' taunt, "he saved others," is, in the eyes of Mark's reader, an ironically true distillation of Jesus' entire mission. Conversely, Jesus "cannot save himself." From the vantage point of the Gospel, Jesus (and the disciple who would be his follower) "gives his life for the many" (10:45), "loses his life to save it" (8:35). The action and words at the Passover meal had condensed Jesus' entire mission of salvation in a similar way and had fused them to his death: "this is my body. . .this is my blood. . .poured out for the many" (cf. 14:22-25). The power of the Messiah was not directed toward himself but towards others, empowering them and making them whole.

The leaders' final words of mockery put the issue clearly before the reader: "Let the Christ, the King of Israel, come down now from the cross, that we may see and believe" (15:32). The leaders propose that Jesus come down from the cross — *then* they will "see and believe." The title mockingly applied to Jesus (but ironically true for the reader) is the "Christ, the King of Israel." The Jewish leaders use the full religious designations "Christ" and "King of *Israel*" for the Messiah in distinction to the politically shaded "King of the *Jews*" used by Pilate. The nature of Jesus' messianic identity has been the deep current of the passion story, especially since the Jewish trial. Now the terms on which Jesus' claim could be accepted are clearly spelled out: "Come down from the cross." As in the previous mockeries, the surface logic suggests that such a miraculous act would be an unimpeachable sign of Jesus' God-given power. Earlier in the Gospel the Pharisees had demanded a similar spectacular sign from Jesus, but he had categorically rejected their "test" (8:11-13). Now they would "test" him again. It is not only a matter of looking for some marvel to validate Jesus' claims. The demand to "come down from the cross" touches again the "scandal" of the cross. The disciples' lack of comprehension, their resistance to Jesus' teaching about the cross, and their eventual flight at the moment of the arrest all amounted to the same proposal: only a Messiah without the cross was believable.

The reference to "seeing" (15:32) is also significant. True perception of Jesus' identity has been the basic issue of the Gospel, one posed explicitly to the disciples at Caesarea Philippi and posed for the reader of the drama on every page. As we have already discussed, Mark uses "seeing" as a metaphor for faith.[86] The mocking proposal of the priests and scribes is, therefore, illusory. They will never be able to "see" or believe in Jesus as he truly is unless they can "see" him on — not off — the cross. The turn of phrase in this mockery, "that we may see and believe," is unique to Mark and is direct preparation for the explosion of events which will take place on the other side of Jesus' death. What the leaders do not see, a Roman centurion will (15:39).

The episode closes with the thieves joining in the derision of Jesus (15:32). The Just One, is utterly alone, abandoned and rejected even by his fellow prisoners (cf. Ps 22:7, "All who see me mock at me").

C) DEATH (15:33-41)

The death scene is the summit of Mark's narrative, the final resolution of the christological issues apparent throughout the Gospel. At the same time, its portrayal of Jesus' stark death is the boldest and most challenging among the four evangelists.

The scene begins with the drawing of a shade of darkness

---

[86] Cf. above, pp. 103-104.

over the "whole land," from the "sixth until the ninth hour" (15:33). The reader is led up to the death of Jesus through a foreboding tunnel of gloom. Mark may be alluding to Amos 8:9 where the prophet describes the atmosphere surrounding the day of the Lord:

> "And on that day," says the Lord
> God,
>   "I will make the sun go down at
>   noon,
> and darken the earth in broad
>   daylight.
> I will turn your feasts into
>   mourning,
> and all your songs into
>   lamentation;
> I will bring sackcloth upon all loins,
>   and baldness on every head;
> I will make it like the mourning for
>   an only son,
> and the end of it like a bitter day. (Amos 8:9-10)

Frightful portents such as an eclipse of the sun at the death of a great personage were stock themes of ancient literature and Mark's reference to darkness has a similar intent.[87] But in the biblical context this sign is not just nature's brooding at the cataclysmic tragedy of Jesus' death. As the Marcan Jesus had already warned in his final discourse such events signaled the endtime, the final days of travail and salvation. "But in those days. . . the sun will be darkened, and the moon will not give its light . . ." (Mark 13:24, quoting Isaiah 13:10). There is no question that, for Mark, the death of Jesus had historic, even cosmic consequences. In this man, and precisely in his death, the covenant was renewed (14:24) and God's long awaited rule had broken into the world.

The arrival of the "ninth" hour (mid-afternoon or three

---

[87] Cf. R. Pesch, *Das Markusevangelium*, II, 493-94.

o'clock) brings the cosmic drama to its peak. The silence of Jesus (since his brief words to Pilate in 15:2) is broken as he cries out with his final lament: "My God, my God, why have you forsaken me?" (15:34). It is the opening line of Psalm 22, which Mark first presents in Aramaic (*Eloi, Eloi, lama sabachthani*) and then translates for his Greek-speaking audience.

The Aramaic form of the quotation suggests that Mark is handing on an archaic tradition that presented the death of Jesus in connection with Psalm 22.[88] It is surely not impossible that Jesus himself in the crisis of death would have prayed this classical prayer of the tormented Israelite. At the very least it can be said that at its earliest stages, the Christian community used the Psalm to express its interpretation of Jesus' death.

The Psalm is a perfect example of the lament form, portraying first the desolation of the suffering Just One (cf. vv.1-21) and then the triumphant vindication of the believer as God responds to his faithful one (vv.22-31). The basic issue of the Psalm and the reason it served so well for Christian reflection on the death of Jesus is the believer's tenacious faith in God in the midst of abandonment and suffering, and the validation of that faith by God's power. As we have seen throughout the passion narrative, Mark has portrayed Jesus as the embodiment of the suffering Just One. Abandoned by his friends, mocked and tormented by his enemies, surrounded by malefactors, Jesus *is* the Just Israelite clinging to his Father, placing his existence solely in God's hands. This motif already had an important place in the passion tradition before Mark. The evangelist incorporates it along with his own more explicit concern with Jesus' messianic identity.

The words of Psalm 22 now serve as the final words of Jesus in the Gospel. Within the context of the suffering Just One theology and of Mark's Gospel as a whole, there can be no question that these words are an expression of *faith*, not

---

[88] Cf. the literature cited above, p. 118, n. 85.

despair or bitterness.[89] The opening line of the Psalm should not be separated from its context of prayer. These words are, in effect, the final version of the prayer in Gethsemane where, also in a "lament," Jesus affirmed his unbroken trust in his Father while feeling the full horror of approaching death (cf. 14:32-42). At the same time, however, the fact that Mark makes Jesus' last words a *lament* must not be downplayed. The emphasis falls on the experience of torment and abandonment. The Marcan Jesus is not the Jesus of Luke's Gospel ("Into thy hands I commend my Spirit," Lk 23:46) nor the Johannine Jesus ("It is finished," Jn 19:30) where a sense of victory and completion brings relief to the death scene. In Mark's account Jesus dies in agony, a wordless scream on his lips (cf. below 15:37). Jesus' trust in God will not be broken, but Mark allows the fierce assault of death to be felt. The lament of Jesus issues from the darkness leading up to the fateful ninth hour (15:33).

Even the final prayer of Jesus is mocked, as the bystanders twist his cry to God into an appeal to Elijah (15:35). They do not simply misunderstand his words, hearing "Elijah" instead of "*Eloi*" (in Hebrew, "my God") but use one final opportunity to torment Jesus. In popular Jewish piety Elijah, as the greatest of prophets and one who had saved the widow and her son in their hour of desperate need (I Kgs 17:1-24), was the "patron saint" of hopeless cases. This seems to be the basis of the taunt. Jesus' prayer to his God is deliberately misinterpreted as a plea to Elijah for deliverance. Continuing the mockery one of the bystanders runs to get a sponge soaked in "vinegar," probably "posca," a beverage composed of water, egg and vinegar favored by laborers and soldiers. The intent may be to revive Jesus, thus prolonging his torment and allowing time for his "rescue" by Elijah.[90] The man's words show that Mark interprets the

[89] See the comments of F. Matera, *The Kingship of Jesus*, 132-35.

[90] This is the view of E. Linnemann, *Studien zur Passionsgeschichte* (FRLANT 102; Göttingen: Vandenhoeck & Ruprecht, 1970), 149-51. F. Matera, *The Kingship of Jesus* 124, prefers to see this as another mockery of Jesus' messianic claims. The bystanders taunt Jesus because they believe that Elijah will not respond to the pleas of a false King.

offer of the drink not as an act of compassion but as mockery: "Wait let us *see* whether Elijah will come *to take him down"* (15:36). It is the same proposal as that of the priests and scribes; once again "seeing" is tied to separation of Jesus from his cross (cf. 15:32). For the reader irony again adds a deeper meaning to the words of mockery. The bystanders refer to "Elijah" as an agent of rescue, standing between Jesus and his death. But the figure of "Elijah" has played a different role in the Gospel. "Elijah has already come" to Jesus not as rescuer from the cross but as a prophetic sign of Jesus' death (9:12-13). John the Baptist was "Elijah," the prophet of the end-time, and his rejection, imprisonment and violent death had pointed the way to the destiny of the Son of Man.[91]

Mark's description of the instant of death is raw and stunning. "And Jesus uttered a loud scream and expired" (15:37). The Greek text is absolutely stark. The words translated as "uttered a loud scream" are literally *apheis phōnēn megalēn*, "emitting a loud cry" or "sound." The Greek verb *eksepneusen* means literally to "breathe out" or "expire." Although various attempts have been made to find in these expressions some direct theological significance such as the "cry" of the Just One in Psalm 22, or a victory shout or even an act of exorcism,[92] it seems preferable to allow the words to have their unadorned brutality. The other evangelists all soften this moment, giving Jesus in death a greater sense of control as he once again prays Psalm 22 and hands over his spirit (Mt 27:50), or dies with the resignation of Psalm 31 on his lips (Lk 23:46) or with a sense of completion and deliberateness (Jn 19:30). But for Mark Jesus dies without such control; he screams and expires. The torments of the Just One have crossed the final boundary. The Son of Man who would give his life for the many (10:45), who would offer a broken body and blood poured out (14:22-24), who would lose his life to save it (9:35), experienced an inglorious death.

---

[91] Cf. above, Part I, pp. 18-22.

[92] Cf. F. W. Danker, "The Demonic Secret in Mark: A Reexamination of the Cry of Dereliction (15:34)," *Zeitschrift für neuentestamentliche Wissenschaft* 61 (1970) 48-69.

No New Testament text more boldly expresses the reality of Jesus' humanity or the manner of his dying. The jackhammer impact of the death scene now shifts radically in mood but not in pace. Prior to the moment of death Mark had presented a picture of unrelieved torment under a canopy of glowering darkness. The atmosphere was pierced by words of mockery, an anguished prayer, and a death scream. On the other side of Jesus' death new portents break out and a new voice is heard. Now there is no mockery or death rattle but an awesome sign of God's power and an acclamation of faith. The tearing of the temple veil (15:38) and the confession of the centurion (15:39), along with the presence of the faithful women (15:40-41), are dramatic counterpoints to the challenges hurled at Jesus prior to his death. If the lament portion of Psalm 22 evokes the mood of the events leading up to Jesus' death, it is the vindication elements in the latter part of the Psalm that coincide with the way Mark describes the aftermath of that death.[93]

The first consequence of Jesus' death is the tearing of the temple veil, "from top to bottom" (15:38). Presumably the veil referred to was that which hung between the inner sanctuary and the "Holy of Holies," a place of absolute sacredness which could not be entered except once a year by the High Priest on the feast of Yom Kippur. Some authors believe Mark refers to the outer veil that covered the temple building itself since this would be visible to the outsider and would encompass the whole temple.[94] Mark does not specify, but the more evident symbolism of the inner veil would seem to make it the likelier candidate.

It seems undeniable that this startling event had important symbolic meaning for Mark, rather than being the report of some historical detail (unconfirmed by any other

---

[93] Typical of many lament psalms, the latter part of Psalm 22 moves from anguish to a sense of victory and exultation (cf. vv. 22-31). In this portion of the Psalm Yahweh is praised for hearing the pleas of the just one (22:24) and the homage of the "ends of the earth" and the "families of the nations" is predicted (22:27-28). Even those in Sheol and coming generations will praise God (22:29-31) for his faithfulness.

[94] See, for example, J. Donahue, *Are You the Christ?*, 201-03.

evidence) or part of Mark's attempt to portray the awesome atmosphere surrounding Jesus' death (on a par with the darkness in 15:33). The reader of the Gospel is aware that Mark has related the fate of the temple to Jesus' death twice before in the passion story (14:58; 15:29) and that judgment against the temple was a strong motif of chapters 11-13.[95] Interpretations differ, however, on the exact significance the tearing of the temple veil seems to play at this point in the narrative.[96] Is the tearing of the veil meant to signify judgment against the temple, the divine presence now absent? Or is it a positive sign, implying new access to God's presence made possible through Jesus' death, not unlike the theology of Hebrews 10:19-20 (where, however, the opened veil is interpreted as Jesus' flesh, a symbolism not apparent in Mark)?

The only sure guide through these possibilities is to keep in mind the meaning Mark has already ascribed to the temple in his Gospel and to pay close attention to the context of 15:38. The Jerusalem temple seems to have primarily a *negative* connotation within Mark's perspective. In chapter 11, Jesus' actions in the temple are a prophetic judgment against it. The words of Jeremiah and Isaiah cited by Mark warn that because of Israel's lack of integrity the temple will be swept away, as Shiloh had been (cf. Jeremiah 7:8-15). In its place would come a house of prayer "for all nations" (Mk 11:17, quoting Isaiah 56:7). In the parable of the vineyard (Mk 12:1-12) the rejection of the Son by the tenants brings judgment on them (12:9), leading to a new community whose cornerstone would be the rejected and obedient Christ (12:10-11). This same motif had been picked up in the trial before the Sanhedrin when Jesus was accused of threatening to "destroy this temple that is made with hands, and in three days I will build another, not made with

---

[95] Cf. above, Part I, pp. 24-28.

[96] Cf. P. Lamarche, *Revelation de Dieu chez Marc* (Paris: Beauchesne, 1976), 119-44. and H. L. Chronis, "The Torn Veil: Cultus and Christology in Mark 15:37-39," *Journal of Biblical Literature* 101 (1982), 97-114; J. Donahue, *Are You the Christ?*, 201-06.

hands" (14:58). The reader knows the ironical truth of these words despite the perjurious intent and confusion of the false witnesses. And on Golgotha the bystanders had hurled the temple word at Jesus on the cross, deriding his claim to messianic authority (15:29). In each of these cases Mark has viewed the Jerusalem temple negatively, as a sign of inauthentic worship and in connection with denial of Jesus' messiahship. In almost every instance it has been directly connected, either explicitly or by context, with Jesus' death.

The immediate context of 15:38 offers nothing to change that symbolism. Unlike Matthew's version, Mark does not present tearing of the veil as part of a series of apocalyptic signs which have at least some positive meaning.[97] Nor does Mark imply that the opening of the veil is what enabled the centurion to make his confession of faith, the splitting thereby having revelatory significance. There is no hint in Mark (again in contrast to Matthew's version) that the centurion (or anyone else for that matter) even knows the veil is torn. What prompts his confession is not such marvelous happenings but "seeing how Jesus expired" (15:39).

Therefore we must conclude that the tearing of the veil is a sign of judgment; it is not "opened" but "torn in two, from top to bottom." The temple "made by hands" has felt the judgment promised by Jesus (13:2). The confession of the centurion and the presence of the women signal the emergence of a new sacred place, the community who lives in Jesus' name. This is a temple "not made by hands." Mark's harsh judgment against the Jerusalem temple should not be interpreted as anti-Jewish, much less anti-Semitic. For this evangelist the temple not made by hands was open to all, Gentile and Jew alike. The Jesus who was the cornerstone of the new temple was the very one who had fed both Jew and

[97] In Matthew 27:51-54 the tearing of the veil is the first in a series of signs that climax in the raising of the dead from their open tombs and the acclamation of the centurion and his companions. Cf. on this, D. Senior, "The Death of Jesus and the Resurrection of the Holy Ones (Mt. 27:51-53)," *Catholic Biblical Quarterly* 38 (1976), 312-29.

Gentile in Galilee and had commissioned his community to do the same.[98]

The chief priests and the bystanders had mockingly offered to believe in Jesus if they could "*see*" him "come down from the cross" (cf. 15:32,36). Their brand of sight, which the Gospel had already labeled as "blind" (4:11-12), is countered by another "seeing" which the evangelist fully endorses. "*Seeing*. . .how he expired," the Roman centurion pronounces the first unqualified confession of Jesus' identity in the entire Gospel: "Truly this man was the Son of God" (15:39). This confession is triggered not by awe at the portents surrounding Jesus' death, nor by any miraculous rescue from death such as Jesus' mockers had demanded but by the *death itself.* The centurion is standing facing the *dead* Jesus (15:39). In this moment the evangelist has pushed his christology to its most eloquent and radical expression.

As we have discussed at some length, the "Son of God" title is one of critical importance for Mark.[99] It designates Jesus' identity as the Davidic Messiah and yet pushes beyond that to express the mystery of Jesus' union with God and his endowment with divine power. Prior to this scene the title had occurred in revelatory contexts as when God had declared Jesus as "Son" at the baptism (1:11) and transfiguration (9:7), or when the legion of demons had appraised Jesus as "Son of the Most High God" come to destroy them through his redemptive mission (5:7). The title had been accepted by Jesus the prisoner when the High Priest had solemnly questioned him before the Sanhedrin (14:61). But nowhere in the Gospel had a human being recognized Jesus' true identity as Son of God in a context of confession. Neither his exorcisms or healings, nor his power over nature had penetrated the blindness of the witnesses. But now, in the ultimate weakness of dying with a scream, in the total giving of life expressed in Jesus' crucified death,

---

[98] On the inclusive nature of Mark's theology, cf. D. Senior and C. Stuhlmueller, *The Biblical Foundations for Mission,* 211-32.

[99] Cf. above, pp. 95-97.

the breakthrough of faith comes: "Truly this man was the Son of God." One can only think of the paradox expressed by Paul:

> [18]For the word of the cross is folly to those who are perishing, but to us who are being saved it is the power of God. [19]For it is written, "I will destroy the wisdom of the wise, and the cleverness of the clever I will thwart." [20]Where is the wise man? Where is the scribe? Where is the debater of this age? Has not God made foolish the wisdom of the world? [21]For since, in the wisdom of God, the world did not know God through wisdom, it pleased God through the folly of what we preach to save those who believe. [22]For Jews demand signs and Greeks seek wisdom, [23]but we preach Christ crucified, a stumbling block to Jews and folly to Gentiles, [24]but to those who are called, both Jews and Greeks, Christ the power of God and the wisdom of God. [25]For the foolishness of God is wiser than men, and the weakness of God is stronger than men (I Cor 1:18-25).

A similar thought breaks out in II Corinthians: "For he was crucified in weakness, but lives by the power of God. For we are weak in him, but in dealing with you we shall live with him by the power of God" (II Cor 13:4). In the logic of human wisdom, the cross is ultimate weakness, definitive mortality. It represents a cause disgraced, freedom taken away, a human life brutally snuffed out. But for Paul, as well as for Mark, the meaning of the cross has been reversed, transformed by the person and cause of the one who is stretched on it and the God who vindicates him. Now the cross means giving of life on behalf of the other, serving instead of exploiting, a broken covenant renewed, life made holy.[100]

---

[100] R. Martin suggests that Mark was intended to be a "supplement" to Paul's thought. By means of narrative Mark is able to give vivid historical grounding to Paul's theology of the cross. Cf. R. Martin, *Mark: Evangelist and Theologian* (Grand Rapids: Zondervan, 1972), 156-62. Whether Mark directly interacted with Pauline theology must remain conjectural but the connaturality between the two is evident.

In the dynamics of Mark's drama it cannot be accidental that the one who makes the Gospel's most profound profession of Christian faith is a Roman soldier, the captain of Jesus' execution detail. Nor is the presence of a company of faithful women noted without significance (15:40-41). The centurion is a Gentile, an outsider within the framework of the Gospel story. He is a sign of the community's future mission. But he also takes his place alongside other "outsiders" who had been magnetized by Jesus' presence while the chosen disciples, the family of Jesus, and the leaders of Israel had remained dull and uncomprehending.[101] The tax collector Levi (2:13-14), the Syro-Phoenician woman (7:24-30), Bartimaeus, the blind beggar (10:46-52), the scribe searching for God (12:28-34), the widow at the temple (12:41-44), the woman at Bethany (14:3-9) had all filled similar roles, warning the reader of the Gospel that "sinners" and outcasts seemed more open to the hidden mystery of the Gospel than the righteous (cf. 2:17).

The women at the cross seem to fulfill a similar role. They, too, are present even if "from afar" (15:40). The glaring absence of the elect disciples and the painful attention to their panicked flight (cf. above 14:50-51) and to Peter's denial (14:66-72) only highlight the women's fidelity. Mark's characterization of the women as having "followed him when he was in Galilee" and "serving him" and "coming up with him to Jerusalem" utilizes metaphors of authentic discipleship rooted deeply in the Gospel narrative.[102] To have followed Jesus from Galilee to Jerusalem serving him, and, above all, to be with him at the cross in Jerusalem are ultimate signs of faithful discipleship.

The naming of these women disciples also prepares the reader for the denouement of the drama. Mary Magdalene and Mary the mother of Joses will witness the burial of Jesus (15:47) and they, along with Salome, will come to the tomb on Sunday morning (16:1). To these women, witnesses

---

[101] On this motif in Mark, cf. below, Part III, pp. 153-155.

[102] Cf. above, Part I, pp. 30-35.

of the crucifixion, the Easter message will be disclosed first. They, too, will be the first sent to proclaim it (cf. 16:7-8).

VII. The Tomb (15:42-47)

The thunderous events on Golgotha give way to a scene that is subdued and sober, an almost anticlimactic finale to the passion story. Yet the burial account serves important functions in the Gospel. It confirms the awesome reality of the crucifixion scene — Jesus is indeed dead. And it prepares the reader for the empty tomb story and the proclamation of resurrection that will bring the Gospel to its close (cf. 16:1-8). In this final act of his drama, Mark begins to show the potent impact of the cross on those "looking for the Kingdom of God."

> 42And when evening had come, since it was the day of Preparation, that is, the day before the sabbath, 43Joseph of Arimathea, a respected member of the council, who was also himself looking for the kingdom of God, took courage and went to Pilate, and asked for the body of Jesus. 44And Pilate wondered if he were already dead; and summoning the centurion, he asked him whether he was already dead. 45And when he learned from the centurion that he was dead, he granted the body to Joseph. 46And he brought a linen shroud, and laid him in a tomb which had been hewn out of the rock; and he rolled a stone against the door of the tomb. 47Mary Magdalene and Mary the mother of Joses saw where he was laid. (15:42-47)

Mark begins by noting the time (15:42): it is now Friday "evening," the day of Preparation for the Sabbath. The evangelist had counted off the passage of time all the way through the passion story: Thursday "evening" (14:7), "cockcrow" (14:72), "dawn" on Friday (15:1), the "third hour" (15:25), the "sixth" hour (15:33), the "ninth hour" (15:34). One final moment is yet to be sounded: "very early, the first day of the week" (16:2), the resurrection day.

A new and intriguing character is now introduced, Joseph

of Arimathea, a "respected member of the council" who comes forward to ask for the body of Jesus (15:43). There is no mention of Joseph any other place in Mark and little real information about him is given here. The "council" (*bouleatēs*) referred to would not necessarily mean the Sanhedrin but, as Luke surmises (cf. 23:51), that is probably Mark's intention.[103] Joseph is presented as a powerful man, of some means since he purchases the linen shroud and arranges for burial in a rock tomb (15:46). Matthew (27:57) and John (19:38) identify Joseph as a "disciple" (although a "secret" one in John's rendition), but Mark offers a more enticing description. Joseph is "waiting for," "expecting" (*prosdechomos*) the Kingdom of God. This suggests that he is not yet a disciple, but is someone open and responsive to the message that Jesus proclaimed (cf. 1:14-15). In similar language Jesus had blessed the Scribe who had instinctively understood and accepted Jesus' teaching on the primacy of the love command — "You are *not far from* the Kingdom of God" (12:34). In both instances a person from the ranks of those who seem to be Jesus' unyielding foes — the scribes and the council — is stirred by Jesus and in so doing moves closer to the Kingdom they seek.

In Joseph's case, however, the context of the passion story adds another dimension. Joseph is drawn to the *crucified* Jesus; he seeks his "body" (*sōma*) an action that involves danger. (Is the reader to think of the "body" (*sōma*) offered at the Passover meal?, 14:22). Note that Mark says Joseph "took courage" before making the request. Public association with a criminal executed for alleged revolutionary activities involved genuine risk, especially for an influential person who may even have been a member of the very council that had condemned this criminal. Therefore Mark portrays Joseph doing something that the chosen disciples had feared to do: he associates himself with the crucified Jesus. The evangelist may leave the reader to infer that the impact of the cross, already so powerfully demon-

<hr>

[103] In 15:1 the Sanhedrin holds a "consultation," the same root word used in 15:43.

strated in the Roman centurion's confession (15:39), is now making itself felt in other unexpected quarters.

Pilate's brief role in the burial story is to certify that Jesus is truly dead. The word "dead" is repeated twice in 15:44 and then confirmed by the centurion (15:45). Pilate is "amazed" at the news since a crucified person could last many hours or even days before succumbing. This emphasis on confirming the *death* of Jesus probably indicates one of the purposes of the traditional burial story, a function it may have in the formula of I Cor 15:3-5, one of the earliest New Testament creeds.[104] Confirmation of death through burial offset theological aberrations which refused to believe that salvation could come through the death of Jesus. It also helped counterattack views which insisted that Jesus had not died but had been spirited away by his disciples, thereby debunking the resurrection.[105]

The burial itself clearly prepares for the story of the discovery of the empty tomb. Joseph removes Jesus' body from the cross and wraps it in a linen shroud he has purchased (15:46). The body is not anointed. Presumably this omission of the prescribed care for a corpse was due to the approach of the Sabbath. The law forbade burial once the time for Sabbath observance had begun (Friday at sundown). But the omission of the anointing also serves Mark's purpose. The reader is aware that Jesus' body had already been anointed through the loving service of the woman at Bethany (14:8). Also the omission of the anointing provides the rationale for the women's visit to the tomb on Sunday morning, after Sabbath rest is finished (16:1-2).

Other details alert the reader to the finale. The tomb has been hewn out of rock. Joseph rolls a great stone before the door, sealing the entrance (15:60), details accurately reflect-

---

[104] R. Fuller, however, discounts this motive in the formation of the burial narrative. The role of Joseph, he suggests, was developed to offset the ignominy of Jesus' hasty burial after his execution in the hands of strangers and opponents rather than his own disciples; cf. *The Formation of the Resurrection Narratives* (Philadelphia: Fortress, 1980), 15-16, 55-56.

[105]. Such a hostile explanation of the empty tomb is directly addressed by Matthew (27:62-66; 28:11-15).

ing the burial vaults used by wealthy families in Israel at this period. The problem of rolling back the stone from the entrance sets the stage for the amazement of the women as they discover the tomb opened and empty (16:3,4).

Mary Magdalene and Mary the mother of Joses, two of the faithful women disciples present at the crucifixion (15:40), take note of the place of burial. Their continuing fidelity to Jesus and their desire to "serve" him (15:41) even now in death, will bring them to the tomb on the first day of the week. That fidelity would be rewarded when they will be the first to hear that the crucified Jesus is now the Risen Christ.

THE END: THE PASSION AS PRELUDE TO RESURRECTION

The long day of Jesus' agony, begun with premonition of death and betrayal at the Passover meal, comes to its poignant, stark conclusion at sunset Friday with his shattered body laid in the tomb.

But in Mark's Gospel the passion of Jesus was never separated from the assertion of his vindication. The Son of Man who would be handed over would also be raised (8:31; 9:31; 10:34). The Jesus who understood he would no longer drink the wine of the Kingdom with his disciples, triumphantly acclaimed he would drink it new in the Kingdom of God (14:25). The passion story, therefore, is also a resurrection story. Signs of that victory were present in Mark's passion account even at its most brutal and barren moments.

It is fitting, even essential, to Mark's theology that the burial story should catapult the reader into the next and final segment of the Gospel drama, the discovery of the empty tomb (16:1-8). A majority of New Testament scholars are convinced that the original and fully adequate ending to Mark's Gospel was the empty tomb story. The longer endings were appended later by other hands to bring Mark's account into harmony with the resurrection appearances

narrated by the other evangelists.[106] But for Mark, the story
of the empty tomb serves as a full-fledged proclamation of
Jesus' victory over death and brings to term the theological
perspectives that have coursed through the entire Gospel.

The women who come to anoint Jesus' crucified body are
astounded to discover the stone rolled back from the
entrance (16:4). Inside the tomb they find a heavenly messenger, a "young man," sitting with authority "on the right
side," and "dressed in a white robe," a garment of victory.
The young man provides the interpretation of that which
the women see: "You seek Jesus of Nazareth *who was
crucified.*" They look, therefore, for the broken body of
Jesus of Nazareth who was defeated in death. But the heavenly messenger announces that a tomb is not Jesus' destiny;
death could not have the last word. What Paul the apostle
called the "last enemy" (I Cor 15:26) had been defeated by
the power of God. Mark's Gospel makes the *empty* tomb the
paradoxical sign of Christian destiny: death experienced
but ultimately overturned.

The words of interpretation are followed by a commission: "But go tell his disciples and Peter he is going before
you to Galilee; there you will *see* him, as he told you" (16:7).
Jesus' promise at the Passover meal is now to come true (cf.
14:27-28). The disciples who had deserted their master in the
crisis of death and Peter who had denied he even knew Jesus
are now to be reunited with the Risen Christ in Galilee. The
Jesus who had led them from Galilee to Jerusalem (10:32)
would now lead them from the city of death and failure back
to the place of mission, the place where they had first been
assembled (1:16-20). There they would "see" him, the term
so vital to Mark's language of faith. In Galilee the apostles
would encounter the Risen Christ. In the pursuit of its
mission, the community would come to see and understand
the meaning of its discipleship. And at the end of time in its
final encounter with the triumphant Son of Man, all of

---

[106] Cf. the discussion in R. Fuller, *The Formation of the Resurrection Narratives*,
64-68; J. Elliott, "The Text and Language of the Endings to Mark's Gospel,"
Theologische Zeitschrift 27 (1971) 255-62.

God's people would "see" the final gathering from the corners of the earth (13:26).[107]
The women at the tomb had encountered the living word of God and finally glimpsed the awesome mystery of the Kingdom. Now they flee from the tomb on their mission, trembling and in "ecstasy" (16:8). What they have seen is unutterable, transcending all human hope. They therefore leave in "fear," gripped by the same wondrous awe that had stunned biblical witnesses from Moses to Paul. The fearful and resplendent presence of the living God was now seen as never before in the crucified Messiah's victory over death.

Now the mission of proclaiming the Gospel to all nations could begin.[108]

---

[107] Cf. more on this notion of "seeing," below, Part III, pp. 151-153.

[108] This ultimately positive interpretation of the women's reaction is at odds with some current Marcan scholars who prefer to understand the women's silence as definitive, that is, they fail to carry out the young man's instructions. Their silence is a final instance of discipleship failure in Mark, and thereby the fate of the scattered disciples is sealed — they never receive the message of Jesus. This is the basic viewpoint of such authors as J. Tyson, "The Blindness of the Disciples in Mark," *Journal of Biblical Literature* 80 (1961), 261-68; T. Weeden, Mark: *Traditions in Conflict*; N. Perrin, *The Resurrection*; J. D. Crossan, "Empty Tomb and Absent Lord (Mark 16:1-8)," in W. Kelber (ed.), *The Passion in Mark* 135-52. However, as we noted above (cf. the discussion of 14:27-28), this interpretation does not do justice to the force of Jesus' promise (14:28) repeated by the young man at the tomb: "They *will see* him in Galilee"(16:7). Also to have the Gospel end on such a negative note would seem to completely subvert the notion of "gospel;" instead of being a story of ultimate redemption it becomes a dark tale of terminal failure and a brutal indictment of Jesus' disciples. For more positive interpretations, in line with what we have suggested, cf. R. Meye, "Mark 16:8 — The Ending of Mark's Gospel," *Biblical Research* 14 (1969), 33-43; R. H. Smith, "New and Old in Mark 16:1-8," *Concordia Theological Monthly* 43 (1972) 518-27; E. Best, *Following Jesus*, 199-207. On the literary function of Mark's seemingly abrupt ending, cf. J. Petersen, "When is the End not an End? Literary Reflections on the Ending of Mark's Narrative," *Interpretation* 34 (1980), 151-66.

PART III

THE PASSION OF JESUS: MARK'S MESSAGE

Mark's recital of the passion story brings to full expression some of the most fundamental motifs of his entire Gospel. To conclude our investigation of the passion, we will attempt to stitch together some of the threads that run throughout Mark's account.

The Passion and Mark's Portrait of Jesus

The passion story clearly becomes Mark's most eloquent statement concerning the person and mission of Jesus. In this story of raw suffering the evangelist's christology, present but often opaquely so in previous sections of the Gospel, breaks into full view.

1. The death of Jesus is the climax of a life for others.

Reading the passion in close connection with the rest of the Gospel demonstrates that for Mark the death of Jesus is the outcome of his messianic mission. Ultimately Jesus is handed over to death not by treachery nor through some arbitrary and inscrutable act of fate. He dies because of the way he lives. As we had noted earlier, Mark prepares for the passion story from the earliest scenes of his Gospel. The deadly plot against Jesus is triggered by characteristic acts of his mission: befriending the outcast, transcending the law in the interest of compassion, laying claim to the messianic hopes of Israel (cf. Mk 2:1—3:6). In Mark's account, Jesus does not choose death; he is intent on his mission of preparing for the coming rule of God. But because that rule means transformation of the human heart and of the social structures the heart ultimately constructs, the messianic mission of Jesus ran headlong into opposition and rejection. Thus while death was not sought it is clearly foreseen in the Gospel.

This inner connection between the ministry of Jesus and his condemnation to death gives the cross an *active* meaning in Mark's Gospel. The passion story should not be disconnected from its moorings in the rest of the Gospel. Martin Kahler's often repeated description of Mark as a "passion narrative with a long introduction" is a half truth.[1] It does point to the dominant presence of the passion in Mark, but the Gospel is not a mere "introduction" to the passion. Rather the passion is, in a very true sense, the *consequence* of Jesus' ministry described in the earlier section of the Gospel. The cross, therefore, is an *active* symbol because it is the ultimate expression of Jesus' commitment to give life to others. The cross is "taken up" not merely endured. Jesus is not a mere victim with death imposed. Jesus chose the way that led to the cross and, as Mark repeatedly states, the cross as a sign of life given on behalf of others is inseparable from the heart of Jesus' teaching. That teaching and mission give redemptive meaning to Jesus' death.

Jesus' commitment to redeeming life is illustrated throughout the Gospel, beginning with his ministry in Gali-

[1]   Cf. M. Kähler, *The So-Called Historical Jesus and the Historic, Biblical Christ* (trans. & ed., C. Braaten; Philadelphia: Fortress, 1964), 80.

lee. He moves energetically to rescue human lives from the grip of evil forces, healing broken bodies, teaching the truth and protecting the weak. He empowers unlikely (1:16-20) and unwanted (2:14) people to change their lives and join in his mission. As the pace of the Gospel drama quickens and the journey toward Jerusalem begins, some of Jesus' most explicit teachings on discipleship portray his mission as one of "losing life to save it," (8:35) of "being the least of all and servant of all" (9:35; 10:44), of "serving rather than being served" (10:45), of "giving life for the many" (10:45).

Thus for Mark "taking up the cross" (8:34) is equivalent to the entire life-giving mission of Jesus. The passion story itself strongly confirms this. As we noted in our discussion of the Last Supper, Mark uses the Passover meal, already laden with liberation meaning in biblical tradition, to proclaim Jesus' death as a redeeming act. His body given and blood poured out, his death, was "for the many" (14:24). It was nourishment for the deep hunger and thirst of human existence. It was a definitive act of hope in the triumph of God's rule over the threat of death.

From Mark's perspective, it is entirely fitting that Jesus is fully proclaimed as God's messianic liberator only in the passion story. Only here where the final act of giving his life is carried out will his messianic identity be recognized. Thus the titles "Christ" and "Son of God" (literally, "Son of the Blessed") are fully accepted by Jesus during the trial before the Sanhedrin (14:62) and, for the first time in the Gospel, someone believes in Jesus as Son of God at the moment of his death (15:34). Jesus is mocked as king and taunted for claiming to be the Christ as he hangs on the cross. But the reader knows that these mockeries are ironically true. The Passion is safe ground for proclaiming Jesus as Messiah because the Passion, for Mark, expresses Jesus' act of loving service for humanity, the authentic meaning of his Messiahship. Thus here, without distortion, Jesus' redemptive mission is revealed.

Mark does not seem to give strong emphasis to Jesus as the Suffering Servant of Yahweh in the passion story, yet this motif is present. The words over the cup which is poured out "for the many," echo a similar phrase in Isaiah 53:12 where the sufferings of the Servant are atonement for the "sins of many". Jesus' commanding silence before the barrage of accusations during the trial (cf. 14:61; 15:5) and the mockeries endured at the end of each session (cf. 14:65; 15:16-20) likewise evoke memories of the Suffering Servant who silently bears indignities for the sins of his people.

By means of these biblical images Jesus' death is clearly proclaimed as a death for others, a death, therefore, fully in harmony with the purpose of his entire messianic mission.

2. In his passage from death to life, Jesus is proclaimed as the suffering yet triumphant Son of Man.

We have repeatedly noted that the mysterious title "Son of Man" is important for Mark's christology. This is the title Mark consistently links with the sufferings of Jesus. Paradoxically, it is also the title that characterizes Jesus' role as the triumphant figure who will come at the end of time to gather his elect and to bring world history to its consummation (13:26). The so called passion predictions (cf. 8:31; 9:31; 10:32-33) combine humiliation and exultation. The Son of Man is to be handed over to death yet after three days will be raised up in triumph. Jesus, the Son of Man, a prisoner before the Sanhedrin, acclaims that the same Son of Man will also come in glory on the clouds of heaven (14:63).

A similar pattern of anguish and glory is implicit in Mark's portrayal of Jesus as the suffering Just One. The Hebrew Scriptures speak not only of the sufferings of this exemplary Israelite but also of the "Just One's" vindication by God. As we have suggested, this Old Testament model may have been already imbedded in the passion story prior to Mark and is handed on without much elaboration by the evangelist. Yet to the extent that he portrays Jesus as one who prays with the echoes of the lament psalms (14:34-36); 15:34), who is betrayed by friends and surrounded by hostile tormentors, the Gospel allows the cloak of the suffering Just One to settle on the shoulders of the crucified Jesus. The expectation of vindication is as essential to this motif as it is the sober account of suffering. If Jesus is the suffering Just One he is also the one God will glorify.

For Mark, therefore, the death of Jesus is not the Gospel's final word. The empty tomb story is essential for understanding the meaning of Jesus' passion. The Gospel is not a tragedy, with the narrative ending in the noble death of its hero. The Gospel is ultimately comic, with the forces of death thoroughly defeated through the life-giving power of God. From the opening scenes of the Gospel, Mark presents redemption as a struggle. After his baptism Jesus is driven into the wilderness to be tested by Satan (1:12-13), a preview of his entire ministry. The first act of his public ministry was to liberate a human life from the power of evil in the synagogue of Capernaum (1:21-28). Throughout the Gospel the most characteristic action of Jesus is exorcism, brawling confrontations with the power of evil infesting human life. From the evangelist's perspective that struggle was never in doubt: the power of God would overwhelm the power of death. But that full triumph, the final exorcism as it were, takes place when Jesus himself feels the full brunt of evil and death in his own body. All of the sickness and oppression Jesus had encountered now seems to be distilled into his own person as he experiences the reality of death. The liberation of the crucified Jesus from the tomb of death proclaims the ultimate significance of the "Gospel of God."

This movement from death to life is, of course, no monopoly of Mark's Gospel but represents the basic proposition of the Christian message. Perhaps the special feature of Mark's account is his emphasis on the *passion* side of the death-resurrection schema. By ending his narrative with the discovery of the empty tomb rather than with the resurrection appearance stories, Mark has shifted the weight of his Gospel in the direction of Jesus' *dying*. Vindication and triumph are sure but they are not narrated. For the reader, as for the characters of the Gospel itself, the full experience of resurrection is promised but not yet fulfilled.

This may be one of the reasons why the Son of Man title is so important to Mark's christology. Son of Man serves as an important complement to other traditional titles such as

Son of God or Christ or Lord. These other messianic titles do not in themselves connote suffering. By portraying Jesus as the humiliated yet ultimately vindicated Son of Man (and, with less prominence, the Suffering Just One and the Suffering Servant), Mark reminds his readers that Jesus' glory was revealed only through a process of dying. Only in pouring out his life for the many was the messianic identity of Jesus validated.

3. Jesus' death is a "theophany," revealing God's power at work in weakness.

One of the most startling and provocative features of Mark's Gospel is that the true identity of Jesus is acknowledged by a human witness only at his death. "*Seeing how he died*" the Roman centurion recognizes Jesus as Son of God (15:39). Conversely only in the passion does Jesus seem to accept without hesitation the messianic titles of "Christ" and "Son of the blessed" used in the High Priest's interrogation (14:63). This clarity stands in contrast to preceding parts of the Gospel where Jesus seems to be diffident about reactions to his miracles, where the disciples themselves fail to understand him and his opponents label him as demonic. In short, the true identity of Jesus as God's Son is manifested not in acts of marvelous power but in an event seemingly devoid of any power, his passion and death.

This aspect of Mark's theology captures a profound Christian intuition similar to that expressed by Paul the Apostle in his Corinthian correspondence: the power of God is manifest in "weakness." In I Corinthians 1:18-31, Paul speaks of the "wisdom of the cross" which is labeled "foolishness" by the Gentiles and is a "scandal" to the Jews (I Cor 1:23). The death of Jesus is dismissed by the non-believers as a wasted life, as defeat, as ineffectual or worse. But God's logic seems to be the reverse of human logic. What is considered "foolish" or "weak" in human estimation becomes an expression of God's power (cf. I Cor 1:25-31). Paul boldly applies this axiom to the Corinthians' own situation. Though they can claim little nobility or clout from a human perspective, they have become an instrument of God's power in the world.

Paul seems to use a similar "Wisdom of the Cross" to reflect on his own experience. The apostle suffered from some unnamed disability, or chronic illness.[2] His pleas to be delivered from it were not answered, but eventually Paul came to a new conviction about his experience of "weakness" or limitation. The power of God enabled Paul to triumph over death: "The Lord said to me, 'My grace is sufficient for you for my power is made perfect in weakness.' I will all the more gladly boast of my weaknesses, that the power of Christ may rest upon me" (II Cor 12:7-11). To the Galatians Paul would express once more the baffling logic of the cross as experienced in his own body: "you know it was *because* of a bodily ailment that I preached the Gospel to you. . . (Gal 4:13). By bearing and transcending what the world would dismiss as ineffectual Paul's own disabled body became the Gospel of the crucified Jesus who conquered death by the power of God. The same intuition stirs beneath Paul's eloquent testimony in II Corinthians, "we have this treasure in earthen vessels, to show that the transcendent power belongs to God and not to us. We are. . . always carrying in the body the death of Jesus, so that the life of Jesus may also be manifested in our bodies." (II Cor 4:7-10).

There are two aspects of this Pauline "Wisdom of the Cross" which are also found in Mark's theology. First of all through the cross God seems to confound human "wisdom." One might expect effective power to be gauged by how much one is able to control events or people, by the degree to which opposition is overwhelmed or suppressed. By most standards, an executed prisoner pinned to a cross is hardly an icon of power or greatness. The cross in human logic spells defeat, humiliation, termination, ultimate failure. Yet Mark's passion story dares to assert that it is

---

[2] Cf. the discussion in K. Seybold & U. Mueller, *Sickness & Healing* (Biblical Encounter Series; Nashville: Abingdon, 1981), 171-82.

precisely here that the most effective moment of Jesus' ministry is encountered. Only here was he fully recognized as God's powerful Messiah. Jesus' cross symbolized the deepest values of his ministry: service, self-transcendence, openness to others. Therefore the cross stands as a sharp challenge to worldly concepts of what is "powerful" or important. God does not work through the grandeur of human might but through the compassionate and tenacious loving service unto death of the Christ. The cross in Mark's Gospel stands, therefore, as a challenge to all abusive and oppressive notions of power.

Another point of similarity with Paul's wisdom of the cross is that Mark's portrayal of Jesus' death as moment of revelation presents a haunting image of God. On three occasions in the Gospel the veil between heaven and earth is breached. At the baptism of Jesus (1:11) and his transfiguration (9:7) God speaks, designating Jesus as his "Son." The events are filled with symbolic expressions of great theophanies: the rending of the heavens, the thunder of divine voices, luminous clouds, and in the case of the transfiguration, the stupor of the witnesses.

The moment of Jesus' death is related to these theophanies. Nature seems to quake as darkness covers the earth (15:33) and the veil of the temple is rent in two. But instead of a voice from heaven we have the testimony of the centurion: "truly this was the Son of God"(15:39). In this instance the theophany is manifested not by a voice from heaven, nor by an angel of the Lord, but through a crucified body. The dying of Jesus on behalf of the many, which Mark narrates with such relentless sobriety, now reveals God's presence to the world. In this unlikely sanctuary, the Roman officer recognizes God's power suffusing the crucified Jesus.

One can only wonder about such a startling theodicy. Again kinship with Pauline thought is instructive. Here is a God who "justifies the ungodly" (Rom 4:5), a God whose "foolishness" is wiser than human wisdom and whose "weakness" is stronger than human prowess (I Cor 1:25). The cross in Mark becomes a "parable" which through strange and compelling imagery dissolves the notion of a God endowed with perfect symmetry and chilling effectiveness. In place of that idol comes the God of the crucified one who stands in solidarity with suffering and limitation. God's voice can be heard in the heart-clutching scream of a dying human being, and the divine presence is felt at the very moment when human hope seems defeated.

Mark's death scene redefines what a "Christian death" must look like. To die in faith need not mean peaceful symmetry, or pious decorum. The Marcan Jesus struggles in death, crying out to God in a piercing lament, and breathing his last with a scream. Yet the God of Jesus is present even —and especially — in these moments when human dignity seems shredded. No corner of human existence is closed to God's presence. No body is too broken, no spirit so bent that the God of the crucified would recoil from it.

The death of Jesus as surprising moment of divine revelation synchronizes with a characteristic of the Gospel as a whole. Thomas Burkill termed Mark's Gospel a "mysterious revelation."[3] Martin Dibelius speaks of Mark as "a book of secret epiphanies."[4] Both labels express an important feature of Mark. Jesus is both present and elusive, instructive and baffling. His touch heals as well as stuns. Time and again the crowd or the disciples themselves react with wonderment and confusion at the words and deeds of Jesus. The Gospel of God which Jesus proclaimed (1:14) is one that comes at an unexpected time and in unanticipated fashion. The Kingdom is indeed "a mystery" as Jesus tells the disciples (4:10). It is a seed growing secretly that bursts into life in a way and at a season the farmer does not expect (4:26-29). Even the faithful women who come to the tomb and receive the message of Jesus' triumph over death, stumble toward their mission in stunned silence (16:8).

In these hushed and mysterious tones, the evangelist not only portrays the obtuseness of the human heart but also points to the awesome transcendence of the God Jesus

[3] T. Burkill, *Mysterious Revelation: An Examination of the Philosophy of St. Mark's Gospel* (Ithaca: Cornell University Press, 1963).

[4] M. Dibelius, *From Tradition to Gospel* (New York: Scribners), 230.

proclaims. God is not predictable or easily domesticated, certainly not a God who saves the world through the death of a crucified Christ.

The Passion and Mark's Portrayal of the Church

The ultimate purpose of Mark's narrative is to give direction to his church. The passion of Jesus, therefore, becomes not only a summation of the Gospel's christology, but, equally important, a distillation of the Gospel's teaching on discipleship and church.

1. The way of the Disciple must be the way of the cross.

Mark's portrayal of the disciples is one of the most tantalizing features of his Gospel.[5] They are the major point of identification between the narrator and the Christian reader because in the glories and failures of these followers of Jesus are portrayed the realities of Christian existence.

As we have noted, Mark assigns certain positive qualities to the disciples. They are called to a unique relationship with Jesus and to a share in his mission (1:16-20; 3:13-19; 6:7-13). They are the privileged witnesses to his ministry and the recipients of his private instruction (4:10-11). They are promised a hundredfold in the community of Jesus and a share in his ultimate glory (10:28-31). Yet alongside these positive notes, Mark seems to give special attention to the weaknesses and even the failures of the chosen followers. They are slow to recognize Jesus, seem to recoil from his teaching on discipleship and tragically abandon that discipleship in the crisis of the Passion itself.

In this remarkably candid portrayal of the followers of Jesus, the reader of the Gospel can trace where Mark sees the Passion intersecting with Christian life.

Mark has cast the life of the disciples as a "journey."[6] The

---

[5] Cf. above, Part I, pp. 31-35.

[6] Cf. above, Part I, p. 30.

"following after" Jesus begins in Galilee with the powerful exercise of Jesus' ministry of healings and exorcisms, then turns radically toward Jerusalem and the cross with the first announcement of the passion at Caesarea Philippi (8:27-31). The arrival at Jerusalem means confrontation with opponents (11:12) and finally the cross itself (14-16). The story ends with a promise given to the disciples through the women who discover the empty tomb: "He is going to Galilee as he told you, there you will see him" (16:7). The journey of the disciples is to continue, back to Galilee, the place of the mission and the place where Jesus will be encountered.

There is little doubt that Mark has given metaphorical meaning to these basic components of the Gospel story. Authentic discipleship is a process that begins with the energy of a divine call, but must also include a long-term process of conversion. In Mark's Gospel the journey to Jerusalem and the passion prove to be a profound crisis for discipleship. Their quest for power, their lack of faith, their failure to be alert in prayer, their inability to understand Jesus lead to a collapse of the disciples' false bravado and to the breakdown of their allegiance to their master and his mission. Inauthentic commitment shatters in betrayal, desertion and denial of the crucified Christ.

The meaning of the cross is, therefore, central to Mark's portrayal of discipleship and its crisis. It is the passion that becomes the "scandal" for the followers of Jesus (14:27). Jesus' commitment to serving rather than being served, his giving of life for the many, is what defines the cross for Mark and it is this core of the Gospel which the would-be disciples find difficult. Their arguments over greatness, and their hunger for dominating power place the disciples in alienation from a crucified Jesus. Conversely, the Marcan Jesus insists that his disciples must "take up his cross" (8:34), must "lose. . .life for my sake and the Gospel's" (8:35), must be "the last of all and the servant of all" (9:35; 10:43-44). These are the clash points between the ways of God and human ways (8:33). And in the glare of the passion the false values of the followers of Jesus are exposed. The fundamental issue of the Gospel, therefore, is the right use of power, the same issue that gnaws at our world today.

Mark's story does not end with failure, however. The crisis of Jesus' death is resolved in resurrection. His giving of life leads to new life. For the disciples, too, Mark's story does not end with the relentless description of their failure but with the promise of their return to Galilee and their encounter with the Risen Christ (16:7). Thus Mark presents the full spectrum of the conversion process essential to authentic discipleship: from the call in Galilee to the purification of false values in suffering and failure, to reconciliation and renewal. The way of discipleship is the way of the cross.

2. The church is, through the experience of the cross, to be a non-triumphant, reconciled church.

If it is true that in Mark's portrayal of the disciples we catch a glimpse of his notion of church, then the passion story gives to that image a sober, sadder-but-wiser tone. The disciples in this narrative are not picture perfect religious leaders. Instead we are presented with people who in the crisis of impending suffering and death abandon their call and flee. Even reconciliation comes not from their own initiative but as a gift freely given by the Risen Christ.

The muted tones of reconciliation, in fact, bring the Gospel to its close (16:1-8). Mark has carefully prepared the reader for this moment. The increasing obtuseness of the disciples on the journey to Jerusalem, climaxing with their sleep in Gethsemane (14:1), is a sure sign of their impending failure. The tragedy of Judas' betrayal had been signaled each time the disciple's name is mentioned (3:19; 14:10,43). At the Last Supper, Jesus had explicitly foretold the betrayal, denial and desertion of his chosen disciples (14:17-21, 26-31). But, as we noted in discussion of this passage, the supper is also a paradoxical celebration of the unbreakable bond between Jesus and his community. Even though they would lose faith in him (14:27) he would not lose faith in them. Death could not sever the bond. So at the meal comes the solemn promise of discipleship renewal: "after I am raised up, I will go before you to Galilee" (14:28). That promise is explicitly recalled by the heavenly messenger who greets the women at the tomb and becomes the content of the first Easter preaching: "Go, tell his disciples and Peter that he is going before you to Galilee; there you will see him, as he told you" (16:7).

The promised return to Galilee completes the journey of discipleship that runs throughout Mark's Gospel.[7] To "go to Galilee" meant returning to the place where the disciples had first been called and where Jesus had proclaimed the message of God's rule in word and power. Galilee, too was the place where the disciples themselves had been sent out and had experienced the joy of mission. But before that experience of following Jesus could be solidified and proven authentic, the disciples had to follow Jesus to Jerusalem and pass through the experience of the Passion. The disciples who would take up the mission of the Risen Christ would be quite different because of Jerusalem. Presumably, their hardened hearts (8:17) would be dissolved; their spiritual blindness healed; their arrogance muted; their claim, "If I must die with you, I will not deny you" (14:31), now a hope rather than a vain boast.

The promise of Jesus speaks of "seeing" him in Galilee (14:28; 16:7). It is instructive to reflect on the sense of that word in Mark's Gospel. Undoubtedly, "seeing Jesus" in the context of the empty tomb story refers to those encounters with the Risen Christ that inaugurated the Christian community (cf. I Cor 15:3-5). Matthew's version certainly seems to interpret the "seeing" promised by the heavenly messenger in this light. Immediately after the women leave the tomb they themselves encounter the Risen Christ who repeats the promise (Mt 28:9-10). The final scene of Matthew's Gospel portrays that promised meeting between Jesus and his disciples on a mountaintop in Galilee (Mt 28:16-20).

---

[7] On the metaphorical significance of "Galilee" in Mark, cf. above, pp. 65-66.

But in Mark's text the "seeing" is not defined and therefore not limited by any subsequent scene. The reader of the
Gospel might be encouraged to think of additional mean-
ings for the "seeing" promised the disciples. Throughout
Mark's story, "seeing" was a major metaphor for *faith* in
Jesus. The opponents of Jesus (4:12) and the disciples themselves were unable to "see" and understand Jesus and his
mission (8:14-21). Conversely the blind Bartimaeus longs to
"see" and Jesus blessed him for his faith (10:46-52). In
Galilee, therefore, the disciples will "see" Jesus. Through the
crisis of the cross the scales have been taken from their eyes
and for the first time these disciples can understand Jesus on
his own terms as the crucified and Risen Christ.

There is yet another "seeing" referred to in the Gospel and
that is the hope-for encounter with the triumphant Son of
Man who will return to gather his community at the end of
time. This is the "seeing" the community must be alert for as
it moves out into history (cf. 13:26; 14:62). The Gospel's
promise directs the disciples to Galilee for this "seeing" too.
In the apocalyptic discourse the Marcan Jesus had told the
disciples that the consummation of history would come only
after the Gospel had been proclaimed to the whole world
(13:10). To seek the end before its time — before the world
had been transformed and renewed by the Gospel — would
be false prophecy. Therefore to "see" the triumphant Christ
the community must return to Galilee, that is, must take up
its mission to the world that Galilee signified.

Thus the finale of the Gospel promises full renewal to the
very disciples who had abandoned Jesus. They will be the
ones to "see" the resurrected Christ and therefore to become
the nucleus of the community. They would now begin to
"see" and understand the mystery of the Kingdom Jesus had
entrusted to them, and they would launch the community
on its mission to the world, a mission that would ultimately
lead the nations to "see" the Christ at the end of time.

But the fact that this awesome promise comes to *fallen*
disciples gives Mark's ecclesiology an enticing atmosphere
of muted joy. It would be hard to read Mark's story of failed
and renewed discipleship and continue to think of the

church as unblemished. It may be that Mark's own community struggled with the reality of failure brought on by persecution and suffering. In explaining the parable of the sower Jesus refers to the seed fallen on rocky soil as those who begin with joy but have no root and "when tribulation or persecution arises on account of the word, immediately they fall away" (4:17). Likewise, the seed among thorns are "those who hear the word, but the cares of the world, and the delight in riches, and the desire for other things, enter in and choke the word and it proves unfruitful (4:18). These texts suggest that failure in discipleship was a reality of Mark's church.

Failure is difficult to accept, especially among those who stand at the center of the community. So, too, is reconciliation. Can someone who has turned away from discipleship be permitted to return? The early church struggled with this issue (see, for example, the uncompromising attitude of Hebrews 6:4-8). It may be that Mark's portrayal of disciples who broke under the cross and yet were restored to full discipleship by the Risen Christ was meant to be a potent message of reconciliation to a church torn with recrimination and factions in the wake of persecution and the failure (as well as the heroics) it generated. Along with the plea for reconciliation implicit in Mark's portrayal of the fallen and renewed disciples is another, equally important, message. The church of Jesus is not a church of infallible humanoids but a flesh and blood church of frail disciples. For such a church to be triumphant or arrogant would be a fatal lapse of memory about its founding story.

3. The crisis of the passion reminds the church that it must be open to outsiders.

This is another consistent brush stroke in the passion story which adds to Mark's portrayal of the church. As the crisis of the Passion deepens, Jesus' disciples falter, and his opponents move in for the kill. But other characters emerge who respond positively and courageously.

The anonymous woman of Bethany anoints Jesus at the

very moment that Judas the disciple seals his bargain with the leaders (14:3-9). Her act of tenderness and homage to Jesus, and her implicit recognition of his impending death are a Gospel witness (14:9). She perceives what the protesting bystanders miss (14:4-5): Jesus is destined for the cross. That perception, as we have noted throughout, is at the heart of authentic discipleship for Mark.

Other similar characters move across the stage of Mark's passion drama. Simon of Cyrene, a passer-by, takes up the very cross from which Peter had recoiled (15:21; cf 8:32). Simon's "taking up the cross" recalls Jesus' own instruction on the cost of discipleship (8:34). Joseph of Arimathea, a member of the council, ends his earnest quest for the Kingdom in the unexpected place of a burial ground, as he finds the courage to reveal his allegiance to a crucified Christ (15:43).

Even though Mark has painfully dwelt on the breakdown of the disciples and their graceless abandonment of Jesus at the arrest, he does not leave Jesus completely isolated at the moment of death. Standing at a distance are some women (15:40-41). There is no doubt that Mark intends to portray the women as faithful disciples of Jesus. The three who are named — Mary Magdalen, Mary the mother of James and Joses, and Salome — will be the witnesses of the resurrection (16:1-8). And all of the women at the crucifixion are characterized as having "followed" Jesus in Galilee, "ministering" (literally, "serving," *diakonein*) him, and "coming up with him to Jerusalem." All three of these designations are metaphors for discipleship in Mark.

The unlikely figure of a Roman centurion is also present at the moment of Jesus' death (15:39). In one of the Gospel's most probing ironies, this Gentile executioner becomes the first person in Mark's narrative to recognize Jesus as the Son of God.

The flight of the explicitly designated disciples and their glaring absence from the climax of the passion story make the presence of these "unlikely" followers of Jesus all the more significant. The community of the crucified Messiah is open to all: the marginal, the rejected, the converted oppressor, those who search for God. This pattern of "unlikely" disciples is found throughout Mark's Gospel. Levi (2:14-17), the Syro-Phoenician woman (7:24-30), the children (10:13-16), Bartimaeus (10:46-52), the scribe who seeks the Kingdom (12:28-34), and the widow in the temple (12:41-44) form a cast of characters whose response to Jesus seems more perceptive and more generous than those disciples explicitly called and explicitly sent out on mission.[8]

This telling contrast between the response of the "insiders" and that of the "outsiders" is an important part of Mark's ecclesiology. The community of Jesus must be a temple open to all (11:17). Exclusiveness and false proprietorship seem to have been a flaw in the disciples (cf. 9:38-41; 10:13-14). The presence of the unlikely disciples challenges such an elitist notion of church. And the tracing of this motif into the passion story itself demonstrates that an exclusivist attitude on the part of the disciples is tied to their failure to understand the cross. Jesus' life was a life open to others; his power was in giving life, not in possessing it for himself. A church unable to comprehend a crucified Christ might be tempted to presume that genuine holiness and sharing in the mission of Jesus were restricted to a few.

4. The church is called to be a living "temple," open to all people and suffused with the spirit of the crucified Christ.

Another motif significant for Mark's ecclesiology which reaches its climax in the passion story is that of the church as temple.[9]

At the moment of Jesus' death the temple veil is torn in two and the Roman centurion acclaims Jesus as the Son of God (15:38-39). Earlier sections of Mark's Gospel help us detect the significance of these portents. Jesus' actions within the Jerusalem temple are interpreted by Mark as prophetic judgment upon inauthentic and exclusive worship (11:12-25).Through Jesus' redemptive death would

---

[8] On these figures as "foils" to the disciples, cf. above, pp. 47-48, 131-132.

[9] Cf. above, Part I, pp. 24-28.

come the possibility of a new worshipping community, one open to all nations (11:17).

The accusations of the witnesses in the trial about Jesus' claim to build a temple "not made by hands" (14:58) and the taunts of the bystanders at the cross in a similar vein (15:27) keep this issue before the reader during the passion. The death and resurrection of Jesus bring the issue to its resolution. The veil before the holy of holies, the inner sanctuary of God's intimate presence with his people, is torn open, a vivid symbol suggesting at once both judgment upon the old and a declaration of new access to God. The ability of the centurion to see God's presence in Jesus' sacrificial death is the first act of worship within the new temple not made by hands. The presence of faithful women at the cross and the new-found courage of Joseph (15:43), as well as the reconciling invitation to the disciples and Peter, mark the first gathering of that worldwide community of the new temple. As Jesus had predicted in telling the parable of the Vineyard, the stone rejected would become the cornerstone (12:10-11), the death of Jesus would lead to new life.

The temple metaphor gives us added insight into Mark's ecclesiology. The church is depicted as awesomely sacred, born in the death and resurrection of Christ. No longer does an inert building contain the presence of God but a living, responsive community. In this community of Jew and Gentile, of men and women, of ruler and outcast is found access to the living God of Israel. This "temple" proclaims the character of its God not by "wonderful stones" (13:1) but through a body broken on behalf of others. This temple's community is not confined to the elite and to self-proclaimed "holy" but is open to the widow, the outcast, the foreigner, the seeker, the repentant.

Once again in this Gospel we discover that the cross enables Mark to redefine the meaning of the sacred.

5. The passion reveals that the redemptive mission of the church is world-wide and costly.

It is evident throughout Mark's account that the passion of Jesus is not merely a singular historic event from the past.

The agony and triumph of Jesus bears cosmic significance and reveals an ongoing pattern of experience that will characterize the church's own mission.

By prefacing the passion story with the discourse of chapter 13, the evangelist prepares the reader for the "cosmic" and perennial nature of the Passion.[10] The sufferings and ultimate triumph of Jesus are a foretaste of the tumultuous mission of the community in history. The disciples are warned of division and opposition (13:7-8, 12-13), of interrogation, trial and torture (13:9,11) as they proclaim the Gospel in Jesus' name to all nations (13:9-10).

Mark sees the community's mission and the suffering it entails as having cosmic significance. The ultimate destiny of humanity and indeed of creation itself will not be achieved until the transforming "good news of God" has touched the entire world (13:9-10). Then, and only then, would the Son of Man come to gather his elect. Any attempt to foreshorten history by proclaiming the Son of Man's advent before the completion of the mission is termed "false prophecy" (cf. 13:5-6, 21-22). Therefore, the travails of the community in history are not meaningless pain nor symptoms of despair but "birth pangs" of a new world (13:8).

The passion story becomes a parable of the community's own struggle in history. Jesus' sufferings are sober testimony to the cost of preaching the Gospel with integrity. His triumph over death is guarantee that human suffering can be the birth pangs of a new creation.

Throughout the passion narrative Mark keeps before the reader the cosmic proportions of the event. Jesus will die at the Passover, the feast celebrating God's final liberation of Israel. In Gethsemane Jesus faces the "hour" of his testing, just as the community must do in the course of its history. The disciples' torpor contrasts with Jesus' prayerful alertness, the stance he had urged upon his community as the climax of history approached (13:32-37). The darkness that envelopes Golgotha recalls the awesome portents of the final age (15:33).

---

[10] Cf. above, Part I, pp. 37-39.

The most overwhelming sign of all is the empty tomb and the heavenly messenger's announcement of triumph. Death's grip on humanity is finally broken: "Jesus of Nazareth who was crucified" has become the "Risen One" (16:6). Birth from death is the ultimate expression of Christian faith and the community's foundational hope as it pursues its mission in history. Mark's passion story, for all of its sober tones, remains a victory story.

The vast proportions of Mark's canvas are important for appreciating the mission thrust of this Gospel. The evangelist does not end the Gospel in a "defensive" or "sectarian" posture. The hostility of the world is soberly assessed. The disturbing potential of the Christian message is not muffled. Yet the expectation of indifference, hostility, rejection and even death, each a component of Jesus' way, does not deter the evangelist from turning the community's attention out to the world rather than in upon itself. The liberating proclamation of God's Good News would continue in the world and on the world's behalf until new life was born. The mission and destiny of the crucified and risen Christ would continue in his church.

SUBJECT INDEX

Abraham, 69.
Absalom, 81.
Alexander, 115-116.
Almsgiving, 45.
Amara, 82.
Amos, 122.
Andrew, the Apostle, 70.
Anonymous Woman (Bethany), 42-49, 52, 105, 113, 131, 134-135, 153.
Anti-Jewish, 128.
Anti-Semitism, 89-90, 128.
apechei (Greek) — "enough", 79.
apheis phonen megalen (Greek) — "utter a loud scream", 125.
Apocalyptic Discourse, 34, 37, 43.
Apostles, 21, 30-38, 43-69, 75-85, 95, 97, 101, 121, 135-136, 148-157.
Call, 18.
arton (Greek) — "bread", 55-56, 58.
Atonement, 142.
Authority. *See* Jesus Christ — authority; Power.
Avarice, 48.

Banquet, 23.
Barabbas, 105-112, 118.
Bartimaeus, 30, 32, 48, 67, 95, 120, 131, 152, 155.
Beelzebul. *See* Satan.
Bethany, 42, 44, 48, 52.
Bethsaida, 32.
Bible — criticism, interpretation, etc., 9-12, 29.
   pastoral theology. *See* Pastoral theology, Biblical theology.
Biblical anthropology, 79.
Biblical research. *See* Bible — criticism, interpretation, etc.

Biblical scholarship. *See* Bible — criticism, interpretation, etc.
Blasphemy, 100.
Blessed Sacrament. *See* Eucharist.
Bread, 54-62.

Caesarea Philippi, 18, 29-34, 75, 95, 98, 121, 149.
Caiaphas, 87.
Call, 149.
Capernaum, 21, 29-30, 143.
Centurion, 48, 92, 97, 115, 121, 126-134, 144, 146, 154, 156.
Charity, 26-27, 36. *See also* Love and ritual; Love Command.
Chief priests, 24-25, 68, 80-87, 93, 106, 109, 111, 119, 129.
Children, 155.
choles (Greek) — "gall", 117.
Christ. *See* Jesus Christ.
Christian Zion, 86-87.
Christianity, 108, 143.
Christians, 37, 39, 48, 113, 120, 123, 131, 146, 155.
   passion, 37, 39, 151.
Christology. *See* Jesus Christ.
Church, 148-156.
Community, 37-38, 91-96, 100, 105, 123, 127-129, 155-157.
   passion of the community, 63, 100, 151.
Compassion, 22, 54-56, 61, 65-66, 77, 120, 125, 140.
Conversion, 149.
Corinthians, 144-145.
Covenant, 60-62, 122, 130.
Creation, 78, 157.
Cross. *See* Jesus Christ — crucifixion;

159

Josephus, 107.
Joshua, 64.
Journey, 30-37, 141, 148.
Joy, 61, 153.
Judas Iscariot, 42-53, 67-68, 80-81, 109, 111, 154.
Judea, 30, 107, 110.
Judgement, 21, 128.
Justice, 8.

kateklasen (Greek) — "broke", 55.
Kedron Valley, 62.
Kingdom of God. *See* Jesus Christ.
Kings, anointing, 45.
labon (Greek) — "taking", *kai labon* — "and taking", 55, 56.
Lament, prayer of. *See* Jesus Christ.
Last Supper, 39, 42, 49-54, 58-61, 120, 133, 136, 141, 150.
Lazarus (Bethany), 44.
lestai (Greek) — "thieves or insurrectionists", 118.
Levi, the Tax Collector, 22-23, 48, 58, 131.
Liberation, 33-37, 44, 51, 53, 58, 62, 80, 110, 130, 140-143, 157.
Passover, Feast of Liberation, 44.
Loaves. *See* Bread.
Lord's Supper. *See* Eucharist.
Love and ritual, 26-27. *See also* Charity; Love Command.
Love Command, 26-27, 133. *See also* Charity; Love and ritual.
Luke, Gospel of, 52.

Malchus, 82-83.
Mark, Gospel of, Theology, 29, 33, 35-36, 38, 47, 52-54, 66, 69, 118, 135, 145.
Martha (Bethany), 44.
Martyrdom, 59, 80, 104, 113.
Mary, Blessed Virgin, 63, 76.
Mary Magdalene, 115, 131-132, 154.
Mary, Mother of Jose, 115, 131-132, 135, 154.
Matthew, Gospel of, 48, 52.
Mercy, 67. *See also* Compassion.
Miracles. *See* Jesus Christ.
Mission, 65-66.
Moses, 55, 58, 60, 64, 137.

Mount of Olives, 34, 37, 43-44, 50, 62, 67, 70, 100. *See also* Apocalyptic Discourse.
Mount Zion, 23.

Nathan, 96.
Nazareth, 18, 56, 63.
neaniskos (Greek) — "young man", 84.
Nero, 104.

Obedience, 76. *See also* God — will.
Obligation. *See* Responsibility.
oidate (Greek) — "understand", "knowing", 103.
Our Father, 76.

Pain, 7.
panta dunata to pisteuoni (Greek) — "all things are possible to the one who believes", *panta...duanta para to theo* (Greek) — "all things are possible with God", *panta dunata...soi* (Greek) — "all things are possible to you", 75.
pantes (Greek) — "all", 84.
Parables, 63, 103, 127, 153.
paradidomi (Greek) — "handed over", 17, 38, 48, 107, 112.
Parousia, 29, 38.
Passion of the Community. See Christians — Passion.
Passover, 43-44, 49, 50-58, 62, 67, 75, 77, 83-88, 102, 110, 116, 135, 141, 157.
Feast of Liberation, 44.
Pastoral Theology, Biblical Theology, 12.
Paul, Epistles of, 54, 79, 146.
theology, 130.
Paul, the Apostle, 54, 73, 79, 137, 144, 145.
perasmos (Greek) — "test", 78.
Persecutions, 37-38, 104-105, 153.
Peter, the Apostle, 19, 29-32, 49-50, 63-70, 77-82, 85-88, 95-104, 119, 131, 136, 154, 156.
Pharisees, 21-22, 56-57, 87, 103, 121.
Philo, 107.
phthonos (Greek) — "envy", 111.
Piety, 27, 73.
Jewish, 73-74, 124.

Pilate, 39, 42, 89, 105-112, 120, 123, 132-134.
Poverty, 7, 46, 75.
Power, 33, 59, 63, 75, 83, 98, 100, 112-113, 145, 149.
Prayer, 67-77, 80, 124, 126, 149.
Lament prayer, 70, 72, 75-77, 124.
Priests, 125. *See also* Chief priests.
proagon (Greek) — "to go ahead of", "lead", 66.
Prophets, 19, 20, 59.
prosdechomos (Greek) — "waiting for", "expecting", 133.
Psalm 22, 123-126.
Reconciliation, 65, 67, 103-105, 150, 153, 156.
Repentance, 24, 64, 104.
Responsibility, 53.
Resurrection of Jesus. *See* Jesus Christ — Resurrection.
Romans, 49, 74, 89, 107-110.
Rufus, 115-116.

Sabbath, 22-24, 44, 88, 98, 120, 132, 134.
Sadducees, 25, 75, 81, 87.
Salome, 115, 131, 154.
Sanhedrin, 81-94, 102, 107-113, 119, 127, 129, 133, 141, 142.
Satan, 35-36, 78, 97, 111, 129, 143.
scandalisthesesthe (Greek) — "fall away", "to be an obstacle", "to cause offense", 63.
The Scribe, 155.
Scribes, 22, 24, 26, 56, 68, 76, 81, 87, 92-93, 97, 106, 109, 110, 125, 133.
"Seeing". *See* Faith.
Servant of Yahweh, 60, 94, 110, 118, 141-142, 144.
Service, 77, 80, 130, 141, 146, 149, 154.
Sheep, 64-65.
Shema (Dt 6:4), 76.
Shepherd, 64-65.
Shiloh, 127.
Sickness. *See* Suffering.
Sidon, 56.

Simon of Cyrene, 114-116, 154.
Simon, the Leper, 42, 44-45.
Sin, 61, 72, 153.
sindona (Greek) — "linen cloth", 84.
Socrates, 73.
Solomon, 95.
Son of God. *See* Jesus Christ — titles.
Son of Man. *See* Jesus Christ — titles.
sosai (Greek) — "save", 119-120.
The Spirit, 35, 74.
Suffering, 7, 33, 37-38, 52, 63, 139, 143, 148, 153, 157.
Suffering Servant. *See* Servant of Yahweh.
The Synoptics, 52.
Syro-Phoenician Woman, 48, 58, 131, 155.

Tabernacle, 23.
Temple, 26-28, 81, 83, 86-87, 90-97, 101, 115, 127-128, 155-156.
end, 25-26.
veil, 126-127, 146, 155.
Thieves, 118, 121. *See also lestai.*
The Tomb. *See* Jesus Christ — tomb.
tous artous (Greek) — "loaves", 55.
Truth, 76, 118.
The Twelve. *See* The Apostles.
Tyre, 56.

Violence, 7, 83.
Vocation. *See* Call.

Widow, 27, 47, 155.
Wine, 54, 61-62, 135.
Wisdom, 130.
Women, 126, 128, 136-137, 148-149, 151, 154, 156.
fidelity, 131, 154.
See also Jesus Christ — attitude towards women.
Worship, 26-28, 92, 155-156.

Yom Kippur, 126.

Zechariah, 64.
Zion, 61.

AUTHOR INDEX

BIBLICAL REFERENCE INDEX